My Kind of
FOOTBALL

MY KIND OF FOOTBALL

By **STEVE OWEN**
Coach, New York
Football Giants

Edited by Joe King

DAVID McKAY COMPANY, INC.
NEW YORK

MANUFACTURED IN THE UNITED STATES OF AMERICA

VAN REES PRESS • NEW YORK

To all those who have worn the Giants' uniform and to all those who have played against them.
—STEVE OWEN

List of Diagrams

My Kind of
FOOTBALL

1

FOOTBALL STARTED TOUGH FOR ME, AND IT STAYED TOUGH. It's a game that can't be played with diagrams on a table-cloth. You have to get down on the ground with the other fellow and find out who is the best man.

It's just like going into the boxing ring with somebody. If you don't beat him he's going to beat you. Football is a contact sport, and that means contact the other fellow a little harder than he contacts you. A good football player will never cry about how hard he gets hit, so long as he gets hit cleanly. He expects that. And he expects to get up and hit the other fellow a little harder when he has his chance.

That's the idea of the game to me. It runs the same as life, which is a kind of contact game too. You can get some awful licks if you live a long time, and if you don't bounce back you're through.

Kink Richards, star back on the New York Giants' 1934 and 1938 world championship teams, had the attitude I'm thinking of. We were working on a new play one day in practice. Richards ran the wrong way and collided with Leland Shaffer, a big, rugged blocking back, hard as granite. Kink was stretched out cold. I thought he was injured. I was uncomfortable, too, because I couldn't spare Richards from the game two days off.

As he came to, I asked anxiously: "Are you hurt, Kink? Are you hurt?"

He stretched himself gingerly, discovered he was still in one piece, grinned up at me, and answered:

"Coach, I'm not hurt, but I'm sure as hell embarrassed."

There is no mystery to football, but no easy way to play it, either. Some teams claim to use hundreds of plays on attack, and that sounds mighty impressive and awful difficult. But fundamentally every football club operates with six to ten basic plays.

All the rest are variations. In fact, the most brilliant set of plays won't mean much if a team cannot gain off tackle. That is the essential bread-and-butter play. Football, as we shall see later, depends on those six to ten offensive plays and on two defenses which can also be varied at will. The game is that simple in conception, no matter how many variations a team may wish to carry.

In my time I have seen the rudimentary game of the early twenties, a smash-and-shove affair of brute force, grow into the streamlined, exciting, scientific, long-scoring football of today. But the fundamentals are unchanged— block, tackle, and practice.

Practice isn't easy. Neither are the hard knocks. The offense of today has to drill until the backs can hit their timing practically blindfolded. When we have gotten a new play down, I ask my backs to run through it with their eyes shut. Our Giants backs actually have run blindfolded in stunts for movie and television pictures.

To stand off the hard knocks a man has to know the art of self-defense, according to the football code, and be willing to employ it. The will has to be there.

Tex Coulter, our outstanding tackle and center, got in an argument with an opposing player during a game in 1951. Tex wore a protective metal mask, but he seldom spoke on the field, and I was interested to know what was going on.

He told me: "This fellow is asking me out, Steve. He's telling me to take off this mask and he'll show me."

I could have only one answer for him: "That's all right, Tex. I want my men to feel free to protect themselves at all times. You handle it whatever way you think best."

The other fellow heard me, and when he learned Tex meant business he cooled out awful fast.

I didn't want big Coulter to fight. But I wouldn't want one of my men to think he had to take sass from anybody. He wouldn't be much of a football player if he didn't have the right and the will to fight back fair and square.

I started in football by knowing nothing at all about it. The longer I've been in it, and the more football I've seen, the more convinced I am there is always plenty more to learn.

Sometimes I get to feeling I am still an ignorant fellow out of the old Indian Territory, after some of my friends play a game over for me and tell me what I should have done. Too bad a coach can play it only one way—on the field. It's wonderful what hindsight will do for strategy.

I met up with football while I was sitting under an apple tree on the campus of Phillips University, at Enid, Oklahoma, in 1918. I was enrolled in the Student Army Training Corps. I had time out from kitchen police and from the classroom, and I was chewing an apple and minding my own business.

The football coach spotted me and came over. He was Johnny Maulbetsch, the famous Flying Dutchman fullback for the University of Michigan. He had graduated in '16, and he was in shape and he was tough. Walter Camp picked him as one of the best in 1914. They told a story at the time that he had crashed off tackle from the two-yard line for Michigan, bolted through the end zone, and knocked over a horse and mounted policeman put there to restrain the crowd.

Maulbetsch said I had a good build and asked if I had ever played football. I hadn't, not to speak of. In high school our kids had heard about the game. We used to stuff straw into a piece of gunny sack for a football, and set to stomping all over one another. We didn't know any rules, and the game was more for the body contact kids love than for anything else. Besides, a fellow could dig his fingers into that gunny sack, and never fumble, and it isn't football when you can't fumble.

I told Maulbetsch I'd never played but was willing to try.

"I think you could learn," he said. "Let's find out. Come on down to the gym and get a suit, and then I'll have about half an hour with you before practice starts."

Maulbetsch didn't teach me all about football in thirty minutes. He didn't try. He got across the main idea—you've got to take a knock and get up and knock back.

For about fifteen minutes I felt he was about to beat me to death. He put me in position and then blocked me down, and when I got up he put me down again. Only the two of us were there, with him thumping me around, trying to show how to tackle and block. He hit pretty hard, and I began to get a little mad.

Once I got the hang of it, I hit him as hard as I could. He didn't get mad. He began to grin. After I gave him a few more heavy jolts, he laughed out loud and called it quits. He had found out what he wanted to know, whether I was a battler.

"You have the idea," he told me. "That's all you need to make a start. It's a rough game and you'll get hurt if you let the other fellow hit you harder than you hit him.

If you are doing the driving, you're not the one liable to be hurt. That's why football is a good game. If any game is worth playing, it's worth playing as hard as a fellow can.

"Football is a game that won't let a man play easy. But don't get the idea it's a roughneck game. Play it clean. You'll learn the rules fast enough. Another thing—I want you to work with everybody on our squad, and have respect for every other boy."

I couldn't improve on that advice for rookies joining the Giants today, and sometimes I get just as big a kick from one of our new men as Maulbetsch seemed to get out of me back there in 1918.

Eddie Price was an example in 1951. He won the ground-gaining title in the National Football League that year by being willing and eager to play his game all-out at all times. He was a name player from Tulane University, brought up as a T formation specialist, but he worked in my A formation, although that was new to him, without a word of complaint. He never thought of an alibi in his life.

Eddie isn't a great big power fullback. He is a well-built boy of 190 pounds, with speed. Nevertheless, he carried the ball more times than any back in the league's history. He had to, because we were short of running backs after Kyle Rote was injured early in the fall. Eddie was bruised and beaten up most of the season, but he was so jealous of his place in the game that he cried one day because he was left out of practice.

I decided to hold Price out of practice in midseason because the boy had become such a workhorse I was afraid he would run himself out. With a sub in his fullback spot one Tuesday morning, we began the drill. But the fellows weren't paying much attention to my instructions.

They were looking over to a corner of the field where Price sat on the grass, sobbing.

I went to him to find out what ailed him. He blurted out that the Giants meant a lot to him, and he couldn't understand why he was left out, unless he was doing a bad job. He thought he wasn't doing a job! Why, no boy could have done more. I forgot about practice for a long time while I talked to Price, trying to convince him that I had so much respect for the job he was doing that I was trying to let him have a rest.

He insisted he didn't need a rest, but I had to make that stick because he was obviously getting too fine. I believe Price suffered while he sat out, because of his fine spirit and pride in his game. I believe he thought it was so awful for him to be taken out of a few signal drills that he played harder than ever in the games. That was one reason why he came back so strongly at the end, to win the title against heavy odds in the last three games when he was marked as the one man the opposition had to stop to check a good part of our shorthanded offense.

Believe me, it was one of the treats of a coach's lifetime to see how the other fellows worked for Eddie, blocking out for him and showing respect and admiration for a game fellow. I know many of our boys felt just as happy as Price did over that ground-gaining title.

I wouldn't have been in football if I hadn't met Maulbetsch, and I wouldn't have met him if it hadn't been for my mother. She was a great one for schooling, while I had the idea I would rather work in the oil fields which were booming down Texas way.

Mother's parents came from the north of Ireland, and settled in Wilmington, Delaware, until they went west to Kinsley, Kansas. When the Cherokee Strip of Indian Territory was opened to settlers, my mother's folks staked a claim a mile and a half from the one my father's people selected. Dad and Mother met for the first time in the Strip in the early nineties, and they were married soon after.

Mother set up the first school in our part of the Strip, near the little town of Cleo Springs on the north bank of the Cimarron River. She taught in a tent in somebody's yard and had six students. She read to me and to my younger brothers, Bill and Paul, night after night before bed and taught us poems. She bought books and magazines by mail for us. She had a keen mind and realized the value of education at that time, when so many people in the raw and rugged country could not read or write. Her one ambition was for us boys to fit ourselves as best we could for whatever we might have to face when we grew up.

I figured I had had a wonderful education when I graduated from grammar school, and I asked to pass up high school. I tried to convince Mother that Dad needed me to help him on the farm. Dad listened to the talking between Mother and me, and then settled the matter. He said: "Steve, you are going whether you want to or not. There has been too much talking. Take out now, son."

Aside from the value of schooling, the two early important lessons Mother got across to me were to respect other people's property, and to treat animals kindly.

We lived about two miles from my Uncle Bert Beckwith. He had twins, Alonzo and Jim, who could be told apart only by close examination of the different scars they got from being kicked while trying to catch wild horses and riding steers. That's the way we played.

One day when they were visiting us, they told me Uncle Bert had shown them how to put out a prairie fire. They asked me to get matches and they would pass on the valuable information to me. I stole the matches, and they lit straw behind Mother's hen house, where she had hens sitting on about three hundred eggs which would hatch out in a couple of days. The hen house was Mother's contribution to the family income.

The twins threw boards on the fire to put it out—that was the valuable information—and sparks scattered over the hen house and burned it down. Uncle Bert began whipping the twins, and I thought I was in for a hiding too. Instead, Mother told Uncle Bert he was wrong in the first place to teach children to play with fire, and to let them go. She took me aside and lectured me patiently on the danger of matches and fire. She pointed out that she had been the loser and warned me never again to do anything which might harm somebody else's property.

The twins were rough on their stock. They mistreated their horses, and I picked up the habit of whipping my horse, which I rode to school. A neighbor told on me, and Mother gave me a dressing down. She told me I would not be allowed to ride if I didn't learn to treat a horse kindly and didn't make sure it was fed and cared for just the same as I would think of food and care for myself.

Between Mother and Maulbetsch I got a pretty good slant on life and on football. The Dutchman was a great one for condition. He talked to us individually about keeping in physical shape. He warned us not to smoke, to eat plain food, and to make sure we had plenty of rest. He stressed the fact that it is fun to play football when you're in condition, and an awful job to go out there when you are not. It sure is.

Maulbetsch worked steadily on me to make me a competent player. I didn't know a signal, or even a punt formation, that first week, but the Dutchman said I would be all right because I had the power, the speed, and the willingness to play. Besides, I weighed 220 and was as solid as a pine knot.

I sat on the bench with the rest of the subs for the first game. There weren't many subs, because the game was slower then and boys wanted to play sixty minutes. I sat next to a tough little Irish kid, Toby Green, an end who never had played either.

The town kids sitting near the bench kept asking why we weren't in the game, and we told them we were too good and weren't used unless the team got in trouble. That seemed a safe enough comeback, because Phillips wasn't having much trouble that day.

In the third quarter Maulbetsch yelled for Owen and Green. I looked at Toby and he looked at me. That was it. We didn't say a word. We ran on the field to learn about football. I found out in the second play, when a guy hit me aside the head and cut my cheek open. I wiped off the blood and said to Green:

"If that's the way they play it, okay. Let's go!"

Green weighed only 165 pounds, but he could hit like a 200-pounder. I played tackle beside him and from there on we just charged and waded into the other fellows every time they snapped the ball, and we knocked down anybody in reach.

Green loved that kind of going, and I caught the fever from him. Maulbetsch couldn't keep us out of the game from that time until we left school. I was reminded of Green a long time after, when Johnny Dell Isola came up to the Giants from Fordham in 1934. He was a jewel of a player, the type who needs no handling, one who suffers when he isn't in the game, and one who just naturally plays with the best when he is in action. Dell Isola was much heavier than Green, at 195 to 200, but they could have been twins for temperament. They were as intense competitors as I ever knew. Neither could stand to be left on the bench.

Dell Isola came to us as a center, when the great Mel Hein was in his prime, which meant Johnny would spend more time as a student of football than he would as a participant. About midseason, after Johnny had played only a few minutes in a few games, he backed me into a corner of the dressing room, planted a finger angrily on my chest, and declared: "I came here to play football and if I don't play more, I am going to quit!"

This kid was not a fresh rookie popping off. He was sincere. I didn't want to lose him or trade him, but I had no spot for him. Hein was an all-time center. But Dell Isola knew that as well as I did and realized he was blocked off from that position for years. I had to sympathize with him, and worry about losing him.

However, Dell Isola calmed down a little toward the end of the year, probably because we were going for the title, and that had to interest him in the team welfare. We played the Bears for the title in the Polo Grounds and beat them 30–13. In the fourth period the crowd swarmed on the field, and a wedge of fans separated me from my bench. Our second-half comeback had thrown the fans into an uncontrollable mood, and we were lucky they didn't try to get in the lineup.

After the game I struggled through the mob and got to the dressing room. I went to each player in turn to congratulate him for his work through the season. I was going to explain to Dell Isola that I was sorry I couldn't use him, and that I hoped he understood I had to go with my best in a title game.

I stretched out my hand to Johnny before I had a good look at him. He was covered with mud; he had a shiner;

he was scratched as if he had taken on the Bears and half the crowd which had come on the field.

He spoke up very seriously: "Steve, I noticed Hein seemed a little tired in that fourth quarter, and I knew that if you could find me in that crowd around the bench you would want me to go in there and give him a rest. So I did." He grinned and added: "I got in a few good licks." From the looks of him, he sure did. I grinned back at Dell Isola, shook his hand, and told him to remember to come back the next year. I couldn't help thinking of Green any time I saw Dell Isola thereafter, and we were lucky to have him a good many years.

After our catch-as-catch-can introduction to the game, Maulbetsch began teaching us the fine points, but he was called into the Air Corps in midseason, and thereafter we had our orders from him by mail. Our captain handed out these diagrams from the Dutchman when we went out to practice. The boys would run through a few plays and then someone would cry: "Aw, let's cut this out and scrimmage."

That went on day after day, with our squad of thirty husky boys hitting each other for an hour or so, and the real game on Saturday got to seem like nothing more important or rougher than another practice.

But I wouldn't advise that kind of practicing nowadays. Precision on plays is too important in the modern game to slight it. Also, in the pros we don't have to scrimmage much. After four years of college a boy has had his fill of scrimmaging while he learns the game. He has the foundation, and he needs polish and savvy after that. Timing is the vital factor in professional ball, and we work endlessly to reach for perfection. We generally don't scrimmage unless it's obvious the boys are losing their sharpness in blocking and tackling. We go back to fundamentals only when required.

Maulbetsch came back from the war for the 1919 season, and, with several good players also returning from service, we had a strong but small squad of seventeen men. The team was known as the Phillips Iron Men, because the regulars seldom wanted out, and the subs had a hard time getting in. That sort of sixty-minute play is impossible today because football has speeded up too much.

I have often been asked why Em Tunnell, our great broken-field runner on punt returns and star defense man, doesn't play on offense too. In fact, I have been bawled out by some fans for not letting Em into the attack.

Tunnell doesn't play both ways, because it would require a superman to work fifty or sixty minutes for twelve games a season and equal the two men on the other side who would play against him in the platoon system. Tunnell is ideally used, to my mind, because he is a master at faking the oncoming tackler into a move and then sliding into the opening, after he receives a punt. On attack he would not have the room to maneuver at the start, which he does in the open on kick receptions. Another thing folks sometimes forget is that a defensive man can be just as valuable to the offense as any of the backs who carry the ball from scrimmage.

Tunnell, for instance, gained more ground for us on kick returns and interceptions in 1951 than any other back except league-leading Eddie Price.

Maulbetsch, with a squad which was not deep enough to provide a varied offense, concentrated on defensive strategy in 1919, and we had an unbeaten year with only six points scored against us all season. Those came in the final game.

Our most important victory was by 10–0 over Texas U.,

which used thirty-five men in the game against twelve for Phillips. We scored ten points in the first quarter and began to dream about rolling up a score. We weren't as smart as Maulbetsch.

In the rest between periods the coach came out and gave us our instructions: "Boys, it's an awful hot day, and they have many more players than we do. If you try for more points you are sure to wear yourselves out, and you'll not have anything left for the end. I think we might have enough points now, if you keep riding them hard on defense. Let's forget offense and kick on first down."

That was sound strategy. We had an Indian on our side, John Levi, who could kick a ball a mile. He did that day, on first down, and we played in Texas territory all the game. With all their men, they found it much too difficult to start around their ten every time and pound upfield.

After that game, a man approached me in the lobby of our hotel in Austin. He said in a surly way: "Guess you fellows feel pretty smart winning that way. How could anybody around here know you fellows had a team?"

I retorted: "You didn't ask me, mister."

He snapped again: "Smart guys, playing us for suckers around here."

"If that's the way you feel, that's the way it is," I said, and walked away.

That was my first meeting with a breed which I got to recognize by sight, or by smell, through the years to come —the tinhorn who bets a few dollars on a team and believes his money buys a lease on the franchise and the right to insult the players and challenge their good faith. I have learned how to handle that breed, which could be exterminated without loss to anyone.

We were able to beat Texas because our coach made sure to give us as sound a defense as he could contrive, right from the start. He realized there would be times when he was outmanned and couldn't count on a bushel of points.

Every team should settle down their defense before getting fancy on offense. You can look much worse losing by 42–24 than you would winning or losing by 17–14 or even by 3–0. The wonderful thing about defense is the steadiness of it. Defense is always with you and is not liable to produce the frequent mistakes and setbacks of offense, which has eleven men against it trying to jam up the delicate works.

Defense is half the game. A team that forgets it isn't likely to win, and winning is supposed to be the object of football. The Giants organized an excellent defensive platoon in 1950 and lost only four games in two years, while handicapped both seasons by injuries to essential ball-carriers.

A sound defense will always give you a breather when shorthanded and even allow an inferior attacking platoon a chance to win by holding the other side close.

Green and I roared through 1919, spilling everyone in sight, and I gained more and more respect for him. I learned from his play that the good small fellows often could do as much damage as men twenty and thirty pounds heavier. The big men might not have the reflexes which combine weight and timing to full efficiency.

The odds are stacked against small men making the major league in football, but some have the fiery spirit and the physical toughness to overcome their grave handicap. I recall Two-Bits Homan, of the Frankford Yellow Jackets, who weighed about 140 pounds but who played halfback as well as a man with another fifty pounds on him. Willis Smith, about 150, was a Giant halfback who had tough fiber in him. Butch Meeker with the Steam-rollers was no more than five-seven and 150, but he played in the roughest company and more than held his own. Another Giant, Tut Imlay from the University of California, weighed 155 pounds but was a genuine first-stringer at halfback. He called our signals, too. How about Buddy Young of the Yanks? And going away back, tiny Joey Sternaman, quarterback for the Bears? From Toby Green to the present day, I have never discounted a small man until he has showed me whether he will or won't do. The answer is always on that field with a football in motion and yardage at stake.

Of course I kidded Green about his weight, and told him he was lucky he had me playing beside him to save him from being killed. But Green could and did handle Tiny Roebuck, 260-pounder, who teamed at the tackles with Tom Stedham on an outstanding Haskell Indian team, one of the most celebrated football outfits of early days. Roebuck was built like Arnie Weinmeister, the all-star tackle of the Giants, and was probably as fast, but Green had him picking himself out of the dirt time and again.

Matty Bell, later so famous at S.M.U., had his first coaching job at Haskell, after he graduated from Centre College, and we played his team. They used to beat almost everybody else, but always had trouble with us.

One of the reasons was that most of us grew up with Indians and played with 'em and knew 'em. We kind of buffaloed them. We knew we had to start out rough and give them a hard deal and we would have no trouble. If we let them get the jump, we were goners. So we would smack 'em as hard as we could for about ten minutes and then settle down to play a game.

Mentioning Indians reminds me of a story of a man who didn't know about Indians. He is George Halas, owner-coach of the Chicago Bears, who founded that great football institution and in 1927 played as well as ran the front office, when we defeated his club for the title.

Indian Joe Guyon, one of the outstanding defensive halfbacks in league history, was on our side. Halas, playing end, floated wide and came up behind Guyon, with the idea of clipping him from behind. Joe heard Halas pounding up, and as George left his feet Guyon turned and fell on Poppa Bear with both knees. Joe then rolled over and grabbed his own knees and screamed.

The referee charged up and called a fifteen-yard penalty on the Bears for clipping. Halas was carried off moaning with two broken ribs. Guyon got up with a look of disgust and said to me: "That fellow ought to know you can't sneak up behind an Indian."

I learned about Indians early in life on the Territory. I couldn't have been more than four years old when an Indian boy chased me down a well. A group of five braves rode into our yard one day, and Dad went out to talk to the chief. I went out too. As the men talked, Indian women and kids came up. An Indian boy made for me, and I ran the other way as fast as I could, and went kerplunk right down the well. Dad had been cleaning the well, and the cover was off.

Dad and the chief hauled me out, and I went into the cabin and stayed there.

After that I realized I had to stand my ground or those Indians would run me out of the county. As I grew up I learned Indians were no stronger than we were and little different from us white boys. We could wrestle 'em about even and do just about everything they could do.

Indians looked like real business in those times. They were still in authentic native dress, and while only a few carried bows and arrows, the rest cradled big old Winchester rifles in their arms when they dropped by. All of them carried wicked-looking hunting knives, about a foot long, in sheaths at the belt.

When I was very small the settlers were wary of Indians, and, even though they got along with them, they were afraid of what could happen and what might happen.

Every now and then there would be talk of their going on the warpath, but they never did, although it was only natural they would flare up once in a while. After all, they'd been kicked around and pushed across the country for years.

Our family lit out of our farm on an Indian scare only once. A neighbor rode up and told us to get packing because trouble was on the way. It was just a scare, but Dad rushed the family onto a lumber wagon with about ten more women and children. The men acted as outriders and rear guard as we drove thirty miles north to safety at Alva, about eight miles from the Kansas border.

We saw a company of U.S. Cavalry now and then, smart-looking soldiers with good horses, blue uniforms, and campaign hats, but their base at Fort Sill was far away, and Alva was the nearest town suitable for defense by the settlers with their trusty Winchesters.

The day the Indian boy chased me down the well Dad gave the chief a cow from our stock, and the braves knocked it dead and skinned and quartered it there in the yard. They offered nothing in return. They had nothing. The buffalo had been killed off, and there was little game for them to hunt. My dad figured it was friendlier to give them the cow, because they would take it if he hadn't.

Dad often said the Indians were on land which they believed was theirs and where their homes had been, and, while they didn't own it any more, he didn't blame them if they resented the settlers and felt as if they had a right to do something about them.

"From their point of view," Dad summed up, "it's just as if we had moved into their front parlor, and most people would get a little riled about that."

But we couldn't afford to let those Haskell Indians get riled in football, or they would sure take it out of us. We had to hit them first, and as hard as we could. We played Haskell the day Dad saw his first game, and he won $120. He didn't know anything about football, but when a fellow sitting beside him said the Indians would run us out of the park Dad asked: "For how much?"

He bet $120, and the other fellow must have thought he had found a sucker, because Haskell had a wonderful team.

We pounded those Indians and scored first, but missed the point and led 6–0. For the rest of that game Haskell never left our territory, but they couldn't make the one big play. It looked as if they would score a dozen times.

After the game Dad came to the gym and handed me fifty dollars, and I asked him what it was for. He answered: "Some smart fellow thought those Indians would chase you out of the county. I knew better. That's your share."

He thought we had beat the Indians 90–0, but the game was harder to defend than the 6–0 win the Giants scored over Cleveland in 1950, a game which created quite a stir because it was the first shutout the Browns ever had hung on them. But the Browns were inside our twenty just a few times, while those Indians hardly ever let us get out of our twenty.

My father was six-two and weighed 230 pounds, and I never saw the day he couldn't take me with one hand and buckle me right down. He was a lover of wrestling—or "rassling" as we called it—horse racing, and hunting.

My father was born in Troy, Missouri, of Scotch-Irish settlers, who had started in Virginia and moved to Tennessee and then to Missouri. Dad worked from boyhood on a big ranch up in Kansas owned by the Rockefellers. He took part in the cattle drives from Texas north to the railheads at Caldwell and Dodge City, Kansas, and he knew the Indian Territory well before it was opened for settlement.

When the rush came, Dad claimed a quarter section of 160 acres near Cleo Springs, in the northwest handle of Oklahoma. It was wild, rolling country, quite sandy, with a little scrub timber in elm, cottonwood, and jack oak, and plenty of the buffalo grass, mesquite, and sagebrush which flourish in dry land.

Our house was in two rooms, one the original log cabin with a dirt floor and the second a board shack attached. It stood in a clearing with that well I spoke of right in front.

The well was significant in those times, because where we lived water was close to the surface and was the inducement to the first settlers to ride far over Oklahoma to get into sand for the timber and water.

The early starters ran over rich, grassy flatland, soon to be worth two and three hundred dollars an acre, to get to the woodland and water. Ironically, the people who came last took what was left and got the best of the Cherokee Strip.

Dad raised cattle, tamed wild horses for riding, and raised corn and vegetables, but he still had to work part time on a neighboring ranch to make a go.

In addition to Indians, we had outlaws in our country when I was a boy. They would pass through on the way to the badlands in the Glass Hills across and south of the Cimarron River.

They often stopped by a settler's house for food. In those days anyone who came along hungry was fed, and no questions asked. In fact, no door ever was locked, and a traveler was welcome to go in and eat what he could find, and pay for it if able. Sometimes we would come home and find money on the table in return for food taken by a visitor we did not know and probably never would meet.

It was hard to tell an outlaw from a homesteader, because all men looked sort of wild. The dress was boots and dungarees and any old shirt, because clothing was scarce and so was money, and Sunday-go-to-meeting togs were out of price. Killing a man in a fair fight wasn't too serious in those times, but stealing a horse was a hanging offense, and we weren't awed by the outlaws, who were mostly highwaymen, stagecoach and bank robbers.

It was a hard country, and there wasn't any fun and games to speak of, except for the dancing every Saturday night. Father played a violin. He would fiddle all night in an old dirt-floor log cabin, with the dust clogging up your nose, and when the collection was taken up it would hardly buy a new string for the fiddle. Once he got six pennies and one button.

Dad played with a Negro called Big Lije, who had been friendly with him since they both worked on the ranch in Kansas. Lije played the guitar and did many other things well. He had staked a claim near us with a lake on it, and it's still there—Nigger Lije Lake.

Sometimes Mother would let me take my brothers, Paul, who was four years younger, and Bill, six years younger, up to Lije's cabin to stay overnight. He told us wonderful tales of the country before the settlers came—of hostile Indians, of deer and buffalo hunting, of the cattle drives, five or six miles a day with five to six thousand head, all the way from Texas to the railroads in Kansas.

Lije was the only Negro in the area, and he fascinated the Indians. When they met him, they were very respectful, and would take a match or piece of wood and fire it and hold the flame between them and Lije. They said they wanted to lighten him up.

Dad sometimes told me the names of the more notorious outlaws, although he would never mention names in their presence. I remember two, Black and Yeager, who gripped my imagination. They looked like the desperadoes in the storybooks I read. They holed up across the Cimarron when they had to, and came over our way now and then for a meal. Sometimes they paid, sometimes not. But they were fair, when they had it. One left a twenty-dollar gold piece one time.

Sometimes the outlaws wanted to trade horses, which was a hobby as well as a business to Dad, and he would spend an hour or two figuring out a deal with an outlaw, or with anyone else, for that matter. Once my father traded six-shooters with an outlaw. He got in exchange one of the first of the Colt .45 double-action revolvers, which my family still has back in Kinsley, Kansas.

Settlers weren't interested in the crimes of the outlaws. They saw a lot of strangers, and each man's business was his own. Everybody was too interested struggling to make ends meet, and it also could be dangerous to be too inquisitive with apprehensive, hair-triggered bad men.

The settlers definitely did not care for the U.S. marshals, who sometimes went through the country in droves, chasing outlaws. The marshals demanded food, corn, anything, and seldom wanted to pay. When it became a practice, it amounted to outright stealing.

A boy wasn't very old in our country before his father

explained to him that he should never ask a stranger his name or where he came from or where he was headed. Dad also advised me to say I didn't know whenever a marshal asked questions about outlaws in our house. He said we were not the judges of these men, nor did we know for sure whether they had even committed crimes. So far as we could see, the marshals did more harm to us than the alleged outlaws.

We judged men by what they did, and not by what they said, in the Territory and when it became the state of Oklahoma in late 1907. That's a pretty good practice for a football coach, too. I have discovered, as they call it, many a good player from a small school, who did not have a reputation, only because I was willing to give him a chance alongside the "name" player from a famous school. I have learned boys are pretty much the same wherever you find them, and that in football boys from obscure colleges often match up to the fellows who get All-American mention, provided they have had sound, fundamental coaching.

In recent seasons we have had two boys who didn't even have college training, yet they were of great help to us. One is Bill Paschal, who played only a few minutes of freshman ball at Georgia Tech, yet who had the ability to win the ground-gaining title of the league twice. The other is Joe Sulaitis, who walked in on us from Dickinson High School, Jersey City, and who became one of the finest all-around players we have had. Joe played half a dozen positions well on offense and defense, and even filled in at T quarterback.

Dad told me the less a fellow opened his mouth, the less he would be inclined to get into trouble. He had a saying: "Never get into a man's personal business. Never ask him how old he is, or how much he paid for anything he's got."

In football it is also a good rule to button the lip. When a player becomes too gabby he is either going to rile somebody up or get a sassy answer back and then lose his head. Either way, he's not much use to the team.

Red Badgro, one of the finest ends we ever had with the Giants, was one of the few fellows who could talk through a game without getting in trouble. He knew how to do it. Red had to block on big Turk Edwards, a great tackle with the Redskins. Turk was such a rugged monster he never was hurt on the football field. But he did turn an ankle getting out of a cab one day!

Badgro told Edwards funny stories to keep him laughing and in good humor, so he wouldn't think too hard about playing football. In one game Red had Turk well under control when I sent in a rookie at right halfback. That kid didn't know how to talk. He got fresh and finally hit old Turk right on the chin.

I took him out and put Dale Burnett back in the position. On the first play Turk rammed into our backfield and stretched Burnett's neck about a foot and a half. When he came to, Dale asked what was happening with Edwards. Badgro said: "That kid came in here and riled him, and now we are in for it."

I learned to take care of gabby guys when I was with the Kansas City Cowboys, my first professional team. I played tackle with Obie Bristow, an Oklahoma Indian, backing up the line behind me. Obie had a tongue too long for an Indian, and he kept inviting the other boys to run through there and see how he would take care of them. Of course, they would have to run over me to get to him, and they did. I had more than enough of this in one game. I stepped back and told Obie that so long as he wanted to get those fellows, he ought to do it first hand, and that he had to play my tackle from then on. After they ran over him a couple of times I let him come back to his old job, and I never heard a word out of Obie ever after.

The best athletes, the great stars, are generally even-tempered fellows who never blow their stacks, because a man who does is the finest asset the other side can have. He loses his sense of team play when he is red-eyed to get at an opponent, and can be racked up. Furthermore, no matter how tough a player gets, he always finds somebody rougher, and then he begins to play dirty to get even. Finally, he is no good at all to his team, because he is disqualified.

And he ought to be disqualified. The rules clearly cover personal contact in football. A man can use his hands on defense, so long as he does not slug with the closed fist or hit an opponent in the face at any time. He can block on attack, so long as he keeps hands in contact with the body and doesn't let an elbow break loose. Any player who twists a man's leg or jumps on a fellow after the whistle or kicks him just doesn't have the temperament for football. A smart coach will get rid of a bad number like that. A man can get hurt in a cleanly played game because football is a risk game. You have to take a chance. Any player who fouls in a way which may permanently injure an opponent ought to be put in jail. If he shows that kind of character on the field, you can bet he's no different at home, or in his business. He oughtn't to be left at large.

Mel Hein, for many years the brilliant center and backer-up of the Giants, was the coolest man I ever saw in football. I saw Hein get mad only once in fifteen years. An opposing fullback did something to Hein and he burned up. The next time that fullback tried to come through, Mel hit him so hard he bounced back through the hole before it could close.

The fullback was carried off the field. That was the only time I saw Hein grim and angry, without good nature on his face.

I have tried to tell how I learned about football, and wanted to put over the point that it wasn't easy. I've known players who thought it was easy and who figured they had it licked without half trying. That kind has to learn the hard way, or they won't do.

A few years ago we had a rookie who was a snorter in his junior year in college but who fell off something sad as a senior. We picked him in the belief we could restore that eagerness for the game he displayed as a junior.

After a few weeks in camp we decided we had failed. The spark was gone. I was just about to release him when he seemed to get on fire. He showed desire again. He went to work. He had an outstanding year and was one of the best rookies we ever had. I wanted to know what made the change in him. He told me he had decided, away back as a junior, that he knew all about football. Eventually he learned he didn't know quite all.

"I wasn't tough enough until it was almost too late," he said. "I am coming back next year to be the toughest man in the league."

He finally got the idea every player must have planted deep down in his heart. It's fine to be fancy, but before you are fancy, and after you are fancy, there is always something which comes first—you've got to give it out and be able to take it.

2

JIM THORPE, THE GREAT CARLISLE INDIAN STAR, BROUGHT me my first contact with professional football. By contact I mean contact.

Thorpe played with the Toledo Maroons, one of the colorful early teams of the game, in 1922. So did Jimmy Phelan, who went on to become one of the most respected coaches in the business. The Maroons barnstormed through the Southwest after the season, and we got together an all-star team of former collegians to play them two games.

The pros beat us in Tulsa on Saturday by 3–0 when Thorpe drop-kicked a forty-yard field goal. I have always accused him of kicking a punt, because nobody could drop-kick a spiral on a muddy field. Thorpe has never replied except with a laugh. Maybe he could drop-kick a spiral in the mud. He could do nearly everything else.

The next day, after an overnight train ride, we beat the Maroons in Oklahoma City by 28–7. We were younger, and recuperated faster.

But Thorpe wasn't too tired to teach me a lesson in the Oklahoma City game. Old Jim played wingback at right half, and I played left tackle. The day before in Tulsa I had been overawed by the great man. I used my hands very gently on Mr. Thorpe and took my time going in.

Jim didn't pay much attention to me and didn't try to block very hard.

The next day I figured Thorpe was getting old and didn't care, so I decided to hike in there real fast and ignore old Jim. I lined up and took off. First thing I knew I was on my back on the ground, with the wind knocked out of me. Thorpe had hit me, and the ball-carrier had gained about fifteen yards through my position. The Indian had shown me a real professional mousetrap.

Thorpe hauled me to my feet and advised: "Son, never take your eyes off their wingback, because he can hit you from the blind side something awful."

Many a game is lost to this day when a green or thoughtless boy plows in there without watching that flanker, for, as Thorpe said, he can hit something awful.

Many a game is lost also through what is called overconfidence, which really amounts to lack of respect for an opponent. Anyone who underestimates the other side in football is in for a good hiding.

You often hear the statement about an outstanding team: "They're just lucky."

I've found out whenever you don't give a man full measure for ability and figure he is "just lucky" you are headed for trouble. When you realize a man may be smart in his profession and not just running a luck streak, and prepare accordingly, you have a much better chance to end his "luck."

I think that's one reason why we Giants have been able to play such good games against the Cleveland Browns. I have known Paul Brown a long time, and never underestimated his ability. Others scoffed at his success at times, but I never did. His club may have been lucky at times, but first of all it was a good club. That kind of club may look lucky, but when you analyze it soundly you will concede success is based on smart coaching and the fundamentals.

It was the same on the field when I was a player. I heard about many a "lucky" player, who was able to get away from blocks and spill the ball-carrier. When I got against some of those so-called lucky players, I discovered they had a great deal of ability.

I learned that from card games back in Oklahoma, too. I've seen fellows rake in big pots night after night and get no more credit than to be called "lucky stiffs." Poker and rummy are common games in Oklahoma, and I used to watch the neighborhood battles. Herb Ustler, a restaurant owner who was the star of the Elks Club, won consistently, but no one thought he was anything but lucky. After studying his play, I concluded he won because he kept them off balance all the time and they never knew what he was going to do with his cards or his money.

That works the same in football. When they figure you are lucky instead of good, they are going to take out after you with a reckless abandon and leave themselves wide open for your counter punch. I'd rather be called lucky than good, because then I know I will have an edge.

At the time Thorpe taught me about watching wing-backs, I had decided on football as a career and was ready to go off to the pros. Before making up my mind, I had a long tussle with the outdoors, with school, and with the booming and exciting Texas oil towns.

My fundamental football education had been completed by two fine coaches, Maulbetsch and his successor, Monty (Tubby) McIntyre, and I was ready for the practical lessons from the masters, such as Thorpe had given me. Maulbetsch and McIntyre gave me a marvelous grounding in the game because they were two different types of coaches. McIntyre, in fact, was the exact opposite of Maulbetsch as a personality.

Johnny was rough and ready. He was always willing to battle for his players, and they had great devotion for him. McIntyre, one of the most brilliant men I ever met, was a smoothie. He was a real strategist from the East. He had previously been at West Virginia and had scored a notable win over the celebrated Princeton coach, Bill Roper.

Mac didn't work us as hard or as roughly as Maulbetsch. He tried to win on timing, precision, and outsmarting the other fellow. I learned lots of football from him that is just as good today as it was in the early twenties. I saw football from two angles with Maulbetsch and McIntyre, and when I started coaching I could put the two of them together, pick out what I liked best, and leave the rest alone.

No two coaches, in my memory of all professional football, could parallel Maulbetsch and McIntyre. Two others, however, with whom I had many pleasant associations, and who were quite different in temperament, were Greasy Neale, who coached the champion Philadelphia Eagles of several years back, and Dr. John Bain (Jock) Sutherland, who coached in Brooklyn and in Pittsburgh.

Greasy was on the lighthearted side when he wasn't on a football field, and Jock held a formal attitude toward people until he knew them well. The three of us had dinner one night, and Greasy made an unguarded remark that I was the only coach in the business he cared for, because I had been his friend for so long a time.

Sutherland never missed an opportunity to tease Greasy, and inquired stiffly: "Am I to understand, Earl, that you don't like me?"

Neale was in a fix, but he met the challenge. He addressed the doctor: "Don't misunderstand me. I think you are a great coach and I have tremendous respect for you. I admire you. But aside from that, I don't like you."

Sutherland roared with laughter.

Many people believed that Jock was a cold man and difficult to know. I thought so until we had talked over football several times. After that we had many pleasant evenings together, and I found him a congenial companion and even lots of fun.

When Jock coached in Brooklyn, he had a very good first team, and so did I, but our replacements were below par. In one game I got my subs up to make a switch at the start of the second quarter. Sutherland did the same. The doctor sent his reserves in first. I had a spur-of-the-moment thought, and held my players around me until play began. Then I sat them down. Our regulars were far superior to the Brooklyn subs and made a touchdown quickly.

This trick disturbed Jock quite a bit, and he said to me after the game: "You will rue the day you did this to me."

When we became friendly, we had many a laugh over that incident.

The Giants have played many of their toughest games against Sutherland teams. He was a great fundamentalist and a sterling teacher of the sport. He played his football hard but cleanly, and if you didn't get right down on the ground with him you had to lose. We did that, and had many great battles, in which the doctor did all right. I think he was probably tougher out there than we were.

His teams gave many a rival the essential lesson that is found in a well-trained team able to block and tackle for sixty minutes. This calls for physical conditioning too, and Sutherland's teams always had a chance to win against higher-rated outfits. The block and tackle can make up for a wide disparity in personnel.

I first met Neale around 1921 when he coached Washington & Jefferson and played baseball with the Cincinnati Reds. Greasy was a great all-around athlete. He played big-league baseball for eight seasons and was a star in football and basketball. He was in Enid with the Reds for an exhibition game and tried to talk me into coming East to play for W. & J. I thought seriously of doing so, because I still had two years to go, but I just couldn't stand against the disappointment my teammates at Phillips showed when I told them about Greasy's proposition.

That fall I was really sick over my decision, because Neale led W. & J. to the Rose Bowl, and I thought at that time that the Rose Bowl was the greatest thing that could happen to a player.

I have known Neale ever since, and always admired him. He did an outstanding job in bringing the Philadelphia Eagles from nowhere to the world's professional championship while he coached them. I have enjoyed needling Greasy as much as Sutherland did. He beat us handily with one of his good teams several years back, and instead of congratulating him at mid-field after the game, I casually remarked that he must feel like a lucky stiff to win such a freakish decision.

That seemed to break his heart. I almost laughed to see his expression of grief. Greasy is sincere and serious about his football, and he began to argue with me right on the field. He insisted that his players were really good ones and that there was nothing lucky in their win that day.

Of course there wasn't, but I was so interested to hear Neale tell me all about his players, their good points and their weaknesses, that I let him talk on about them every time we met for the following month. After all, we had to play the Eagles again. We did a little better the second time, but couldn't lick them. After that, I admitted to Greasy that he was not a lucky stiff, and that I had only kidded him. He seemed profoundly grateful to hear what was only the truth.

I was always able to get a rise out of Greasy. When the clubhouse man told me he had suffered a mild heart attack after one of our games in Philadelphia, I figured he would worry himself nigh on to death unless someone got him thinking of something else.

I went over to his clubhouse and began abusing him to get thoughts of his condition off his mind. He gave the abuse right back to me, and when the ambulance came he got up indignantly and walked out to it, with a parting remark for me. He was healthy again the next day. Later I felt sorry about that scene but only because a Philadelphia writer, who didn't know my purpose, blasted me in the paper for abusing Greasy while he was ill and "helpless."

Maulbetsch had left Phillips after the 1920 season to accept the coaching job at Oklahoma A. & M. Before he left he made sure that several boys who wanted to go to a bigger school selected his alma mater, Michigan. McIntyre coached us in '21 and '22. Under him we became a scoring team. Maulbetsch had built his strategy on toughness and scrimmaging and defense to get us through an unbeaten season. McIntyre led us to an unbeaten season in '22 by teaching the use of speed to run around the other fellows, and we averaged a point a minute.

McIntyre never failed to think of a trick or two to disconcert the other fellows and put them off guard for the play he had in mind. The week before we played Central State Teachers he gave us a fancy lock-step shift, which hadn't been seen before and may not have been seen since. But it served his purpose for the game.

We figured to beat Teachers easily, but Mac somehow believed we might have a hard, rough game at the start, because Teachers considered that the state title was at stake. He also made sure we had no idle time to become overconfident, because we were busy learning that shift all week.

First time we received the ball, the three linemen on each side of center stepped back a pace and faced right. Each man put a hand on the shoulder ahead of him and the six linemen lock-stepped four paces toward the side line. Then they wheeled left and stepped up one yard into the line. That put all six men together with the center on the end. In the meantime the backs had lock-stepped four paces before taking new positions.

On the first play one of our backs went forty yards to a touchdown, but we were called offside. On the next play the same back went forty-five yards. McIntyre's shift had paid off to get us the first score. The Teachers' defense collapsed from acute bewilderment, and school was out. We won 44–0.

The lock-step shift drew a good deal of publicity in the local papers. The following Friday I worked as an official in a high-school game near Enid. The team apparently had read about McIntyre's success with his shift, because the linemen went into a lock-step first pop.

But—those linemen just circled around their backs and returned to their original positions, while the defense looked on in wonder, but not in bewilderment. I have often thought the "shift" I saw that day had about as much sense to it as many a freak "variation" I have seen in later years, which usually confused the fans and never the opposition.

In 1923 I was assistant coach to Monty McIntyre, but we both left after that season. His father died in Martinsville, West Virginia, and he went back there to take up the practice of law.

I went off to the pros, determined to stick to football as long as I could. I had licked the oil fever, along with the hankering to roam the outdoors which was always in my blood. Big towns didn't agree with me for a long time. Our family grew up in a country where a city fellow was a novelty. Not that we didn't know how to take care of city slickers. That came naturally back there in Oklahoma. I remember one time I was teaching school in Binger, Oklahoma, after the Giants' season closed, when several traveling men met me in the lobby of the hotel and suggested a little poker.

When they called me "professor," I knew they thought they had hooked a live one, so I said I didn't mind if I did play. I hadn't grown up in that country learning to take care of myself against Indians, rough-and-ready kids, tough hombres in the oil fields, wrestlers, and pro footballers, for nothing. It wasn't for nothing. Those traveling men saw me in the lobby the next day and they didn't bother to invite me again.

I never was used to sitting still until I got to the New York Giants. When I was a boy back home in the Strip, we had just trails, no made roads. Today you'll find the eighty-eight-mile Turner Turnpike and over the Arkansas a half-mile bridge that cost $30,000,000. But in the early days a trip to Alva, about thirty miles, was a two-day affair, one day up and one day down. It was there I received from my dad one of the finest presents I ever had. I couldn't have been more than three when he bought me a brand-new western saddle, with a horn in front for roping and a cantle in back for more comfort. It was the envy of the neighborhood for miles around, and I guess in time every kid around learned to ride in my saddle.

Dad moved a few miles over the Oklahoma line into Kiowa, Kansas, when I was six. The Kansas Kiowa was the end of the Santa Fe Railroad at that time. (There is also a Kiowa, Oklahoma, ten miles south of McAlester.) It was the place where Carrie Nation began her goings-on with a hatchet in the saloons. But I recall at least one saloon-keeper there, a fellow named Cunningham with a huge handle-bar mustache, who was a real frontier character. He wore light hats and checked vests, with a big watch chain and an elk's tooth on the waist. I remember him because he tried to promote good will among the home folks by passing out candy to us kids.

Dad bought a livery stable in Kiowa, because of hauling to be done from the railhead. I went to school with a boy whose father owned the other livery stable in town. Almost every day at lunchtime we would start wrestling over whose father had the best stable, and most generally we would miss eats entirely.

I earned my first money in Kiowa. The jail, a bare, one-room building with bars on the one window and one door, was in an alley back of the main street. When the hands cut up too much of an evening, the sheriff would round 'em up and poke 'em into the jail.

They didn't mind at night, but when they got up in the morning with a hangover, and the sheriff left 'em alone until ten or eleven o'clock, they were moaning for a drink of water. Mother was so sympathetic she couldn't stand it, and she hit on the idea of filling a teakettle with water, so that the snout would fit between the bars. She would let me take the kettle to the jail whenever there had been a big evening, and the poor fellows were so happy to see

[37]

that snout they would throw out halves and silver dollars to me.

I was the top kid of unique distinction in Kiowa for a while, until Mother disapproved. The old colored man who drove the garbage wagon took a liking to me, and let me ride with him. Then he trusted me to drive the team, which set all the other kids green with envy. I was driving down the main street one day and spied Mother and hailed her. She didn't drag me down from the seat— Mother was the gentle kind—but she busted up the garbage-truck romance right away.

After a few years Dad traded his livery business for another in Valley Center, a few miles north of Wichita. This was a rig barn instead of a hauling stable. Traveling men would put in there and hire a rig to go visit their customers.

A fight wasn't far off when we got to Valley Center. The first day there we put up at a hotel. The son of the owner, Spec Carnihan, was pretty much the bully in the town, and it wasn't two hours before he asked me into the alley. I had been used to a lot tougher kids than Spec knew, and I gave him a lacing. That not only got me off good in Valley Center but put Spec on my side in whatever I wanted to do. Spec was the first one I ever knew who put the old maxim to use: "If you can't lick 'em jine 'em."

When I was thirteen, Dad decided to move back to the Strip. He traded his stable for a string of horses. These were better-bred horses, all three or four years old, and Dad realized how valuable such animals would be over in Oklahoma.

Back we went, and Dad began breaking the horses and selling them in teams. Then we stocked up with cattle and mules. I went to county school, running or riding the two miles, doing my chores in the afternoons, and playing baseball on Saturdays. I played with the Hood family of seven brothers, all rugged characters. Their dad played with them, so the team was the Eight Hoods and Owen. These kids were so tough they would break the ice in Nigger Lije Lake in winter and go swimming. I wasn't that tough. But they never bothered me. This time I had joined the right side.

As I grew up Dad traded horses with me from time to time, usually giving me a younger one for an old one. We would do that as a game. He would tell me I couldn't ask him the price of his horse, and he couldn't ask about mine. He would preach to me that a man had to be proud of his judgment and stand by it, and bet on it against the other fellow's judgment. So we looked over each other's horses and made our trades. He never did tell me at any time which of us had the better of a deal. It was up to me to learn. He wanted me to learn to go with my own judgment, without help and without second guesses.

That trait of my father's, which I adopted, paid off in football, because I learned never to be hoodwinked or glamorized, I guess you would call it, by a reputation, until I had seen what was behind the reputation on the field.

Just going along with my own judgment, as Dad had taught me, brought one of the all-time Giants to New York. I went to Dallas to see Marquette play Texas Christian University in the Cotton Bowl on New Year's Day, 1937. Sam Baugh was with T.C.U., and Marquette had the Gueppe twins and Ray Buivid. The Gueppes and Buivid got all the headlines for Marquette in the Cotton Bowl game, but to me a fellow named Ward Cuff did all the work.

I went back to the dressing room after the game, and

[39]

the Marquette coach, Frank Murray, said: "Who's on your mind, Buivid, or is it the Gueppes?"

"Neither," I told him. "I want to see that Cuff."

Murray seemed puzzled and asked me why Cuff was my man.

"Because he did all the work out there today."

He said: "Surprises me. We didn't think Cuff was much."

"Maybe you didn't see him from the stands, as I did," was my last remark before going over to Cuff. I signed him. He proved to be one of the league's finest players and one of the best men in the long history of the Giants.

Mother bundled me off to Aline to high school, and I lived at my aunt's house there, and came home week ends. I graduated in three years, because I went to summer classes at the State Teachers College at Alva.

We had a basketball team in high school. I played guard —stationary guard. We didn't have a regular court, but got permission to play in the city hall. This was a long narrow room with a roof only four feet above the baskets, a stage at one end and a door in the other. We would get those outside teams in there and just tramp 'em to death.

Our captain, Bus Brown, was our center, and a good shot with either hand. The principal was our coach, and when we had a particularly good season it didn't take much talking to get him to enter us in the state tournament at Phillips U., in Enid, which later was to be my alma mater.

In order to get to Enid we had to go to Carmen, Oklahoma, seven miles away, to catch a train at 4 A.M. Brown's father hitched a team of mules to a wagon and started out with seven boys at 1 A.M.

We won the first game and kept right on winning. In the final we met the Enid team. The Phillips gym was a great big place compared to our bandbox. We were able to win by setting me back as the hatchet man. I stood in the circle under the basket, and anyone who came in there did so at his own risk. There was more than a little contact in basketball in those days. We won that final game by 17–14, and came home in style. Many of the fans from Aline were at Carmen when we arrived in the morning, and we were driven home in cars.

Our boys just didn't know what it was to get beat. Brown was a fine leader who kept us battling. We guarded very close and the others didn't get many shots. Brown was our big scorer, but I seldom got past the middle of the floor.

I went into oil during one of the summer vacations. Somebody started a wildcat well about three miles from our house. There wasn't any reason for it to be there. Somebody just had an idea you could find oil anywhere. From the discovery in 1901, the oil industry had boomed. Cushing field, only fifty miles to the southeast, was yielding over 300,000 barrels daily. I worked twelve hours a day for three dollars, as a roughneck on the derrick floor, helping the driller of the rotary rig. Though we found no oil, the work fascinated me, and when I graduated from high school, I didn't want to go to school. I wanted to go to Texas. I had the oil fever.

I worked at a number of odd jobs, including the wildcat oil well that fall and winter, but when we got into the war in 1917, Mother said it was time to have a talk. She told me I would have to go into the army, and that she felt it would not be right if I didn't try to become an officer. She pointed out I had an education better than most boys of my age at that time, and therefore I was better equipped to begin studying for officership. She won that argument, and I enlisted in the Student Army Training Corps, from which officer candidates were selected.

Ten minutes after being sworn in with four hundred others at Phillips, I was hustled off on kitchen detail. It was not a very glamorous start on becoming an officer. There was nothing fancy about that deal. We took the subjects they wanted us to take. We drilled early in the morning, went to class until 3 P.M., and then had a couple of hours for recreation. After dinner they marched us into the study hall for two hours at night. They didn't trust us to study. They set us there and made us.

The war was over when our first season under Maulbetsch ended, and most of us packed out of school. We couldn't wait to leave. I went to Texas that spring and summer. Maulbetsch wrote and outlined to me the benefits of coming back to school. Mother wrote, too, but she no longer insisted that I go to school. She left it up to me. She was betting on my judgment.

But it wasn't easy to go against the action of the oil country. I was in Burkburnett, just north of Wichita Falls, a boom town of about 7,000 population which grew to 100,000 in ten days after the oil strike. It was a wild frontier town of easy money on one hand and poverty and hunger on the other. The riffraff from half of the country dropped by. Chiselers, gamblers, hijackers—all toting guns and ready to shoot. There were many shootings. Only one thing can happen when you carry a gun in a tough town— you get in trouble. I never carried a gun in my life, excepting for a shotgun on the farm to hunt quail and rabbits.

Burkburnett was a town of one-room shacks, board walks, and knee-deep mud. Cars, trucks, and carts were stuck all over town. There were holdups and knifings any time of the day or night. There were burlesque shows, saloons, and gambling dives. There were no roofs on some shacks—only side walls. Drunken roughnecks had just reached up and pulled off the roofs. It was like a gold rush movie, and it had to have the appeal of excitement and action to a young fellow.

One of the workers in my gang had a streak of white hair plumb in the center of his head, and because of that he was called Skunk. He was a rig builder who drove twenty-penny spikes. Whenever he got on the warpath it was time to stand clear. If he ever hit you with that nailing arm of his, you would topple over. When he got high flying he would walk into a joint, announce loudly he was Louisiana born and Texas raised and looking for a fight. Everybody would scatter.

I worked for a contractor named Bull Angus. When his wagon got stuck in a sock hole one day with a big load of pipe, he got out and whipped his team. I whipped him for whipping the team, but he didn't take it amiss. One fight more or less didn't matter down there.

I worked with a crew of five, who all weighed two hundred or better and who could move like halfbacks. We took pride seeing how fast we could do the job. In the oil fields speed is worth money. When you are changing bits you go as hard as you can, then rest. You work two hours wringing wet and then rest up four or five hours.

One of the first drillers I worked for used snuff. He carried it in a little can, and when he took a pinch he always stepped around the corner of the derrick, out of sight. I went out to tell the fireman I thought the fellow was taking dope and might run wild.

The fireman had about as much sense as I had, because the two of us watched the driller carefully for a week, to find out what he was taking. Finally he threw a can away and we read on it—"Snuff." I became a friend of his after that, and learned about snuff from him. His name was Bob Hawker. He was born and raised in the oil fields and was a great driller, called on for trouble jobs.

There was danger in oil too. Fire was a grave hazard, and I was close to it more than once. I saw lightning hit a storage tank, and I watched 50,000 barrels worth five or six dollars a barrel go up in smoke. Nothing could be done about it.

I worked days and I worked nights by the lights of the yellowdogs, the flares of waste gas shooting out of little pots with two snouts on 'em. It was dirty work, but thrilling. We worked in mud and in oil, but first thing we did on location was build a blow-off steam box to wash clothes, and a shower bath. Khaki pants get paler and paler when they are steamed and steamed, and a roughneck isn't a man of distinction until his pants are almost white, with the dark oil stains in 'em.

I sure had oil fever. I even thought of prospecting on my own. At one time I had some leases on land that turned out to be dry. All the roughnecks had the ambition of getting a rig and going into contracting. During those days in Burkburnett oil stock was sold on the street corners like ice cream cones. Most of it was worthless. People bought city lots, expecting the land was big enough to be worth while. Slickers poked around everywhere trying to do somebody out of a well and peddle it.

Don't know how I left it. Oil had a grip on me. But as fall came around I thought more and more of that football.

About the first of September I walked in on Mother. She didn't act surprised at all when I told her I was going back to school. I didn't tell her I was going back to Phillips for football and would have to take the schooling along with it.

I was never sorry I left the oil fields. I never saw a gun yet that wasn't made to go off. And I figured I wasn't smart enough to make a fortune in the gambling halls. As it was, I came home with enough money to pay my way through school. The oil fields were a soft touch for a young fellow who had that in mind. Otherwise, oil was tough, hard, and at times a bitter life.

Football looked especially bright to me that fall of 1919 because Maulbetsch had returned from the Air Corps, and because Dutch Strauss, our fullback, also was out of service. I never saw a better fullback than Dutch, who later became editor of the Enid *Daily News*. He weighed 220, and could run end, hit the line, kick, pass, and back up. He was just my size. We could wear the same clothes from shoes to shirts, and I guess we did now and then. Dutch and I became pals and decided to go in the pros together. We got the chance after that series of games with Toledo in '22, which brings me back to where I opened the chapter.

A fellow named Johnson, who was a baseball umpire in the American Association for years, operated the Toledo football club. He signed Strauss and me to a contract for 1923 at fifty dollars a game. When Monty McIntyre heard of it he asked me in for a talk. I lacked about twelve hours of college credits for a degree, and Mac pointed out how foolish I would be to leave before I qualified. He sympathized with my desire to continue in football, and offered to take me on as his assistant coach for 1923. In that way, he said, I would have an idea of football from the coaching angle, which would be helpful when I moved up to the pros. I agreed, and backed out of the Toledo deal. Strauss was a little miffed about it, but he understood my wanting the degree, and left on his own.

The experience with Thorpe had fired my imagination,

and the year with the ingenious McIntyre, as his aide rather than as a player, excited me even more about the possibilities of football.

For the first time I saw the whole picture. I realized I had gotten only the grounding in the business. I appreciated how much I had to learn. Things began to open up for me under Mac's patient instruction, and I got the hang of what really went on in a game. I guess you might say I had been only in tactics as a player and that I was moving into the over-all strategy as an assistant coach. Now I was ready and eager to become a pro, to learn at first hand how the great coaches and best players put out in a game.

I couldn't grasp then how fascinating a world I was about to enter. I couldn't, for instance, imagine seeing a tackle of the inventiveness of Link Lyman, one of the all-time greats, who played for the Bears. At that time defenses were set, but Lyman was a guy who was never set. When I played against him first, I wondered what he was up to. He would move, or drift away from his guard, and make it very difficult to block him. He moved here and there, sometimes coming in to jam up against his guard, rather than splitting.

Should you move out with Lyman? If so, you leave a gap. Should you stay inside? If you did, you were placed exactly right for them to undress you on a running play. I didn't know it then, but what Lyman invented was the first move in the complicated defensive maneuvers of modern times. His tactics in splitting from the orthodox spacing of the line was the forerunner of a vast new code of practice in the mechanics of both offense and defense.

I often quizzed Link about his invention. He said he had struck on it almost unconsciously, as an instinctive move to fool a blocker. His style and innovations impressed me so much that a seed of an idea was planted in my mind. This finally led to my own device, the A formation attack which the Giants used to win the world title in 1938.

I didn't know when I went off to the pros I was going to see the winningest end I ever knew in my life, Guy Chamberlain, who played with the Canton Bulldogs and later coached the Frankford Yellow Jackets. In every close game I saw Chamberlain play he was the guy who caught the pass, picked up the fumble, or recovered the blocked punt for the decisive score. The way he could change a game with his speed and alertness was uncanny.

But Lyman and Chamberlain and the great parade of stars I have seen in the National Football League seemed a little further away in 1923 than in '22, because I didn't have a job. Toledo had folded, and I didn't know who else would want me, or how to go about it.

Strauss came to the rescue. He had hooked on with the Kansas City Cowboys after Toledo flopped. He got me a job with LeRoy Andrews, promoter of the Cowboys. In August of 1924 Dutch and I set out from Enid in an old Chevrolet coupe for Kansas City, 350 miles away. We didn't have paved roads in those times, and we drove for three days to reach Kansas City. That was a long trip. I didn't know it was only the start of a longer trip which has kept me in professional ball for more than a quarter-century.

3

I REPORTED TO KANSAS CITY IN 1924 FOR $50 A GAME. Nowadays I understand the standard asking price of boys fresh out of college to be around $10,000, and that some of them get that much and more. There's one measure of the growth of the game in little more than twenty-five years. Pro football was a baby when I first began playing for money. It was an infant that seemed pretty near an orphan to us from time to time in those early years.

Linemen worked for $50 and $75 a game, when they were paid, and the very best sometimes got as much as $100. Backs went for $125 to $150, although there were rare cases of well-known stars who got $250. Occasionally a fellow with top publicity value would hold out for $300 or $400 and get it—but only for a game or two.

Some clubs, and I mean entries in the National Football League, would go along with local boys as guards for $15 to $25 a game until the chance came for a good crowd, when imported "high-priced" $50 guards were hired for the day to increase or please the crowd. Nowadays, even linemen are recognized as part of the game and are paid well.

Money was always scarce for the pros in the twenties. Passing the hat was a common occurrence at games in smaller cities. Curly Lambeau, one of the pioneers of the game and one of its most famous figures, often had to solicit contributions to raise eating money for his gang.

Today there is no hit-or-miss about it. The home club in the NFL guarantees the visiting club $20,000 per game, rain or shine, and even that does not cover the average weekly cost of putting the club on the field. Back in '24 only a few teams could afford to offer guarantees for a full home schedule. Most tried to wangle traveling money instead from a richer club, and if that was not possible the team was idle.

There was a club representing Hammond, Indiana, in 1924, which never played in Hammond. Doc Young, a colorful figure of the time, picked up a team in Chicago and took the name of Hammond. The men stuffed their gear in their football pants and were off to the races, but not to Hammond.

The league was a makeshift affair, changing from year to year, with no formal schedule, and with certain clubs playing fewer games than others. The NFL was in its fourth season in 1924, and this was its lineup of cities: Cleveland, Chicago (Bears and Cardinals), Frankford (Philadelphia), Duluth, Rock Island, Green Bay, Buffalo, Racine, Columbus, Hammond, Milwaukee, Akron, Kansas City, Dayton, Kenosha, Minneapolis, Rochester.

Two years later, when I moved to the Giants, Cleveland, Rock Island, Kenosha, Minneapolis, and Rochester had dropped out, and the following cities had come in: Pottsville (Pennsylvania), Los Angeles, New York, Providence, Detroit, Hartford, Brooklyn, Canton, and Louisville.

All told, forty-three cities of varying sizes have been represented in the league since 1921, and only three clubs have held uninterrupted membership, the Chicago Cardinals and Bears, and the Green Bay Packers. The Giants, with the longest membership in the East, joined in 1925.

The league is set up in two sound divisions today, with Cleveland, Pittsburgh, Washington, Philadelphia, New York, and the Cardinals in the American Conference, and Green Bay, Los Angeles, San Francisco, Dallas, Detroit, and the Bears in the National Conference. The winners of each division meet in a postseason game for the championship.

You will note that Green Bay is the only small city still remaining, of the dozens which tried to maintain franchises. I hope the Packers can stay in the league forever. They have one of the finest traditions in football, made by many teams on a par with the best through the years, and they are a tribute to the civic pride of their small Wisconsin city.

The game of 1924 was one of hard knocks, and little finesse. Jim Thorpe was still the terror of the league, and there were many tales about his power and ability. There was a catch phrase, "Never turn your back to old Jim on a pass."

That's because a few fellows had tried it on short buttonhook passes, and old Jim had laid into their kidneys with those big and heavy old-fashioned leather shoulder pads he wore. Thorpe, who had switched from disbanded Toledo to Rock Island with Little Twig and Pete Kalac of the Carlisle Indians, put Gus Dorais out of football with such a tackle on a hook pass.

Thorpe's shoulder pads would not be permitted today. Equipment was rudimentary in that period and offered little body protection. For instance, the hip pads and thigh guards were sewn in the pants, and when the pants became old and sagged, the pads fell away and did not guard the vulnerable kidneys.

Our pads now are of foam rubber or kapok on the inside, with a hard leather cover. They fit snugly around the top of the hip bone, to prevent bruises, cover the kidneys, and protect the base of the spine. Shoulder pads are of the same composition and are webbed so that the force of a blow, distributed evenly, seldom settles on the bone point. The helmet is on the same order—foam rubber inside, hard leather outside, and webbing to spread shock evenly.

Equipment manufacturers now have attained a high safety factor, and the only absolutely vulnerable part of a player's body is the knee. No gear can be designed to protect the knees against sudden pressure from all angles in clipping, tackling, blocking. Knees are more trouble than any other part of the body.

One of the roughest areas in the country for football years ago was the coal sector of Pennsylvania. I guess it still is. There were four very active towns in that territory —Shenandoah, Pottsville, Gilberton, and Coaldale—and not a blade of grass in their league. These clubs often hired the biggest men they could find in the mines, without regard for experience. Mike Palm, my backfield coach for some years, had many a hair-raising experience in the "coal league."

"We were playing Coaldale one time," Mike related in a yarn-spinning session some years ago, "and they had two old fighters, Honeyboy Evans and Blue Bonner, on their side. But we had Frank Kutzko, who looked like Bull Montana and who was three times as big, if you can imagine that.

"Kutzko picked up Harry Robb, of Coaldale, and slapped him down on that rocklike ground. I objected; I wasn't as big as Kutzko. 'They'll take it out on us, Frank, if you don't lay off,' I told him.

"He answered: 'Mike, this is football. If I can kill him, I will kill him!'

"Things got rougher from that moment, and it was only a question of time until the crowd mixed in as they often did. But it was a close game. We were ahead, and they were holding off to let their guys try to score.

"As we got down to those last few minutes, I recalled that we had to go down an alley to dress in a firehouse, and that the alley would be just like running the gauntlet if the crowd reached it first. I warned our fellows, and with about half a minute left I faded and tossed the ball as far downfield as I could. Then we took off at a gallop and beat the crowd to the firehouse. We left when the crowd cooled off, and got out of town fast."

That story is typical of the way many a game was played when I first began to see the country with the Kansas City Cowboys. Once in the iron ore district of Minnesota, one of our ball-carriers was in the clear running down the side line. Two rough customers came out of the crowd, wrestled him off the field, and knocked him out on the edge of the bench. It would have been worth the referee's life to give us the touchdown. He called the ball dead where our fellow was kayoed.

It was a rough-and-tumble and dangerous game, and far from the precision game of today.

The important thing to remember about the early days is that the pros brought the game to people who had no chance to see the college game. Football in colleges was only beginning to move toward the tremendous scope, gigantic stadia, and importance it held years later. It was not easy to get to a college game. Our early barnstorm teams filled the gap, and, in doing so, they improved from year to year and created a great mass of fans who became rooters for all of football, whether high school, college, or pro.

When Dutch and I reached Kansas City, we were lost in the shuffle at first. Others were on hand with big college names. They got paid all the way up to $150, and they came first.

LeRoy B. Andrews, our coach and promoter from Pittsburgh College, Kansas, had gathered a fine group of players for those times. Pro football was just getting established in the West. Fellows from the Big Ten were beginning to treat it seriously, and coaches were coming from the East with the latest ideas. Andrews had men drawn largely from the Big Ten, Missouri Valley, and Southwest Conferences, and some were well enough known to be crowd-pullers in the territory Andrews hoped to tour—from Kansas City to Pittsburgh.

The nearest pro team to Kansas City was Rock Island, Illinois, and Andrews therefore had a fertile field out our way for obtaining players. He also had to buck a public which wasn't too willing to pay money to see football. They just didn't know much about it, and they might or might not become curious enough to find out what it was about.

Andrews ran the club on a shoestring, but to my knowledge he never beat a boy out of a quarter. He had the confidence of all. Sometimes he failed to meet his weekly payroll. Then he would pay off most of us on Sunday night, and come around Monday to borrow back what he needed to pay the rest of the team. When he hit a good game he could catch up with all of us. I wouldn't have known about that practice if Andrews hadn't told it on himself when he came to New York to coach. He had often asked me to loan him back half the fifty he had given me, which I was always willing to do because that many dollars went an awful long way in those days.

Andrews didn't take long to find out he could do without a few name boys in order to make room for two Swedes and Owen. Some of the name players hadn't taken the knocks those two Swedes and I had absorbed growing up. We just couldn't afford to flinch and didn't.

The first Swede, Milton Rhenquist, showed up our second day of practice in the Blues' Park in Kansas City. He had on work shoes and overalls. He weighed about 240 and had heavily calloused hands. Andrews was willing to give Rhenquist a tryout, and he set him to scrimmaging against one whole side of our regular line, without pads. The Swede just battered the hell out of us for one solid hour, never saying a word. It wasn't scientific, but it sure was effective.

The fellows got tired of being slapped around by Rhenquist. One gave us all a laugh when he quit and told Andrews: "Don't worry about that fellow, he's all right." Our boys had begun to worry about themselves.

Andrews offered Rhenquist the standard beginning price of $50. The Swede snapped it up fast, and you could see sorrow on the coach's face for going so high on his first offer. But Andrews was a quick thinker, and added: "Of course, for that fifty you have to take care of the baggage on the road." Rhenquist agreed and played center, guard, or tackle on demand, and for sixty minutes if needed.

This Swede stayed with Andrews when he moved to Cleveland and Detroit and finally to the Giants as coach in 1929. Andrews brought over many of his finest players from Detroit in '29, notably Bennie Friedman, one of the first and greatest forward passers. He also brought along a blocking back, Tiny Feathers, who was as tough a man as I've ever seen. He was nothing short of hell's fire on a block or tackle. Rhenquist coached LaSalle Academy in Providence for a while, and is still up there working in a prison and coaching on the side.

Another Swede named Berquist from Nebraska came in shortly after Rhenquist, and I never did learn his first name because he was "Swede" right from the start. Berquist was built just about the same as Rhenquist and was just as hard. When we had that pair of 240-pounders planted at the guards in the standard seven-man line defense of the time, the opposing ball-carriers had to forget the middle, because trying to run over the Swedes when they got set down there on hands and knees was just about as tough as beating your head against stumps. As a tackle, I appreciated both the Swedes. It was nice and companionable having either one next to me.

Those Swedes had little or nothing to say on any subject. Generally they were satisfied to act, and not talk about it. But one speech by Berquist did cost us a game. We played in Rock Island in our second game, and were marching two, three, four yards at a clip toward a winning touchdown late in the game. We went about sixty-five yards to their ten-yard line when Berquist, with victory in sight, stood out in front of us, raised his hands, and shouted: "Come on, fellows. We shall not be denied." It was one pep talk that didn't work. Our backs got to laughing at Berquist's unexpected and unprecedented outburst and they fumbled.

Andrews put me in as a regular after the first two games because I proved to be in better condition than several name tackles he had hired. I could work the job sixty minutes without losing my speed, and was faster anyway down field under kicks. The way Maulbetsch and McIntyre taught football it was just unthinkable for a player to get out of shape. Also, I had built up pretty good stamina through wrestling.

Oklahoma is a famous wrestling state, and I was in on the beginning. When I was at Phillips, Ed Gallagher was starting the sport at Oklahoma A. & M. Gallagher probably did more for intercollegiate wrestling than any other man, and I was of some help to him. I had been a pretty good neighborhood wrestler, and Gallagher invited me along on his basketball trips, to meet one of his men between the halves as an added feature. I never got the best of those matches. It might have been because Gallagher always insisted on serving as referee.

My dad started me in wrestling, because he liked it, and would match me with the biggest kids in the neighborhood without ever asking me. It got to the point where I had to be good in self-defense. One time Dad came home with a huge Greek. I was a big boy, but the Greek must have had about fifty pounds on me. Dad told me he had got into an argument about wrestling with the Greek, and had bet him that I could throw him.

We lived in the country, and there was no such thing as a mat. So we got out in the sandy yard and took off our shoes and shirts. I estimated I had more stamina than the Greek and could lick him if he didn't get hold of me too fast. I kept him moving around for about an hour. This used up a lot of valuable stamina, and he lost enough stuff for me to handle him.

Dad applauded: "Nice work, Steve. I knew I wasn't wrong." All Dad had done about being right was sit on the side lines looking at the show.

About that time wrestling was a popular side line in traveling carnivals in Oklahoma. The customers were invited to earn ten dollars for staying ten minutes with the carnival bruiser. I often won the sawbuck, and never passed up a carnival if I could help it. One day I over-did it.

That was the time Maulbetsch took us into Waco, Texas, to play Baylor in 1919. We arrived late Friday, and I dropped by a neighborhood side show, hoping to pick up a few dollars wrestling. I got my chance right away, and earned the money. I felt proud because, spying Maul-betsch among the spectators, I had put out extra hard.

Next day was about as hot as it gets in Texas, and when we took a long lead into the second half I thought Johnny would let me off for the day. He kept me in for the full time. When the game ended, I was scorched and parched. Maulbetsch explained, innocently: "When I saw you wrestling the night before a big game, Steve, I thought you'd be glad of another chance to work off excess energy."

When I became a fair and dependable professional wrestler in my first few years with the pros, the promoters in Enid, Wichita, and Oklahoma City would ask me to fill in if they had vacancies on their cards. I used my own name, and also the assumed name of Jack O'Brien.

I worked with Scissors Joe Stecher a number of times. I wrestled the semifinal to the big Strangler Lewis–Stanis-laus Zbyszko match in Wichita. I guess I could claim the championship of Oklahoma, because I always could beat the man who claimed it. He was Link Decker, a huge Dutchman out of Lahoma, Oklahoma, who couldn't wait for me to come back home from football to challenge me. He never beat me, but one time I worked out a month before I would tackle him. It's a good thing I did, because the first fall went forty-six minutes.

To this day, Link says when he sees me, "I have a no-tion to tie into you." I always reply: "If you do, I'll half kill you," and then we both laugh. Neither one of us would dare let the other get a hold. Something might snap.

By the way, don't get the wrong idea about my wrestling career. I don't mean the act they pass off today as wrestling. Ours was honest-to-goodness wrestling, which I guess is about the dullest sport in the world to watch. Get two good, experienced men on the mat—fellows who know how to get the fall once they have a good hold on the other fellow—and you are likely to see them on their feet for thirty to forty-five minutes, fencing each other for that fatal opening. It's not spectacular, but tough and scientific.

Andrews drilled us Kansas City Cowboys in the Blues' Park, but he couldn't afford to put up the guarantee for many home games. As a result we spent most of our season on the road in my two years with him, through 1925. We went to Milwaukee, for instance, for our opener, because that club had offered us transportation and a share of the receipts. The colorful Jimmy Conzelman was then beginning his long career in the pros with Milwaukee.

My first meeting with Conzelman had an interesting sequel, and a surprising one for him. In 1928 he coached the championship Providence Steam Rollers. He was the dude of football, and appeared on the bench in doeskin vest, spats, and cane. He was a slim, handsome fellow, and to look at him you would take him for a dandy, and not the tough football player and terrific competitor which he was.

But the story concerns a trade he made with the Giants that year. Milton Rhenquist went over from the Giants to the Steam Rollers. Next time we played, Conzelman called me aside.

"Owen," he began, "I wish I knew that name a month ago. I wanted to get you from the Giants but couldn't think of your name. I remembered so well what you looked like. I described you to Doc March, but he sent me

Rhenquist. Well, there's not much difference between the two of you in looks. At least not enough for me to claim foul or wrong deal. And he's a good man, too. However, I promise not to forget your name again, Owen."

He didn't, and I always had cause to remember his. We were coaching rivals through the years until Jimmy won another world title, with the Chicago Cardinals in 1947, and soon after retired to private business.

We wandered from Milwaukee to Green Bay, Chicago, Duluth, Rock Island, and Racine. That first trip was really an eye opener to a fellow who had never been out of Texas and Oklahoma.

When Andrews ran out of bookings now and then, we just sat where we were, hoping the money held out, until he could fix up something by telegraph. We toured dressed in chaps, boots, and cowboy hats. Our outfits and background were a good selling point for publicity when Andrews talked business. Our players hailed mainly from Nebraska, Oklahoma, and Kansas, and, while they were good, they were unknown to the teams, writers, and fans in eastern areas. It wasn't until 1925 that we got to New York.

Our boys were all rugged characters who went out to stomp down the opposition. We hated to be taken out of the game. That amounted to an insult. Even if they were hurt, our boys would try to cover up. There were reasons why football was more of a sixty-minute game then than it is now. No one had thought of specializing in offense and defense as it is done—and overdone—in the two-platoon arrangement. There wasn't much need for defense experts, because the forward pass was not yet a deadly weapon. Play was limited to a small area of the field. As a result, squads were small, sometimes as low as fifteen men and seldom more than twenty.

Another reason: there were no such liberal or free substitution rules as there are today. If a man went out in the first half, he couldn't come back until the second half. And if he left in the second half, he was out for the day. Obviously, if a coach didn't have a deep squad, he had to play at least half of his squad for sixty minutes. That made it a slow game, with little resemblance to the raceway-speed sport of the present.

We almost lost a game when I was with the Giants because we waived the substitute rule to allow Ernie Nevers to return to the game. This all-time great back of the Chicago Cardinals had been hurt in the third period and taken out. The Cards claimed they were shorthanded for the fourth period and asked if Nevers might return. Why not? We were leading 14–0, and besides, Nevers was hurt.

All Nevers did was score two touchdowns in six minutes and kick one extra point. When he missed the final point that would have tied us, a Giant said: "I was wondering where that guy was hurt. He's been raking hay all over us since he came back. Now I see. To miss a point like that he must have been hurt in the big toe!"

I finally got to New York because Andrews had run out of games in Duluth in November of '25, and Tim Mara, owner of the Giants, offered to pay to bring us east. We thought ourselves lucky in being able to load up with sacks of ham sandwiches and pack into a day coach for the long ride to the big town.

Andrews couldn't afford cowboy regalia that year, so he hired outfits for us whenever we got to a big town. In New York we rented the stuff from a costumer and dressed in Mr. Mara's office in the Knickerbocker Building overlooking Times Square. We were all big men, and the elevator operator sure looked us over when he gave us a lift. When we came down decked out in all that wild west gear, his eyes popped. It seemed as if he was ready to take off and let us take over the town.

We gave the Giants a hard game, but they beat us 3–0. Dutch Hendrian, who now plays gangster roles in the movies, was the bad man for us with a field goal. I was thrilled to see New York, because it never had entered my mind that I ever would. I never expected to again, but a year later I came back there to stay.

The Cowboys finished the season in the east. From New York we went to Hartford, Connecticut, where we checked into a fine residential hotel, carrying our uniforms, with the jersey stuffed in one pants leg, and the sweat shirt in the other, so the shoes wouldn't fall out. That's the way we traveled, light on the baggage. The uniforms were seldom cleaned. That was almost impossible, because of the way the lower gear was designed, with hip pads, thigh guards, and pants in one piece. All we could do was let the mud dry on the breeches, and then use a wire brush to make the pants lighter in weight, but hardly any cleaner.

Nowadays if a team doesn't wear clean, smart uniforms it doesn't, and shouldn't, attract fans. Appearance today must meet the highest standards of show business as well as neatness and cleanliness.

For an idea of what the well-dressed football player wears now, here is what each Giant receives for the season: sweat socks, outside stockings, hip pads, shoulder pads, thigh guards, shin guards, pants, numbered jersey, rib pads, and helmet, for what you might call battledress, and, in addition to this, training gear consisting of short pants, warm-up jacket, rubber jacket, and sweat suit.

The only unfamiliar item to the fans may be rib pads. These are foam rubber or other type of resilient pads hung over the shoulders to protect the ribs. They are not worn by all players, but chiefly by blockers and ends who otherwise would take a bruising in the upper torso.

Out of curiosity I looked up the cost to the club of uniforms. It is $135 per player. We buy forty uniforms at a time for $5,400, and as each player must have a change because of laundering time, and for relief in rain or mud, the uniform outlay per season runs to $10,800. Players buy their own shoes, which cost $16 to $25.

A player today can feel proud of his equipment, but I wasn't proud in 1925 when we walked into that hotel in Hartford with those filthy uniforms slung over our shoulders. I overheard a lady remark to a group in the lobby:

"Those are fine-looking, strong young men. It's a pity they never had the chance to go to school."

I guess she thought we had just come in from the range and had never seen concrete sidewalks or tiled floors.

It was the custom then to dress at the hotel or rooming-house for the game, because locker rooms in most places offered scant accommodations even for the home team. There were no such things as equipment trunks, which could be packed into the park with all our outfits and gear.

I always felt ashamed, as I did at Hartford, to walk into a sparkling lobby with a dirty and often muddy uniform on me. The custom continued in football long after necessary, and I tried to break it wherever I could.

When I was invited to coach a Blue–Gray postseason game in Mobile, I was amazed to find the habit still prevailing, although dressing rooms were entirely suitable. I got my team to dress in the park. I think that provides a lift to morale, being able to take a shower and walk out and leave that stuff behind. My dressing rooms have to be scrubbed and tidy. The surroundings can have a harmful effect on the attitude of players. They are impressionable anyway, and dirt never put anybody in a happy frame of mind.

After we played in Hartford a fellow named Mulligan from Waterbury asked me to play on a team to oppose the famous Four Horsemen of Notre Dame and an all-star cast in a series of exhibitions.

We played games on four successive Sundays in Hartford against the legendary quartet, Stuhldreher, Miller, Crowley, and Layden. After that, I packed my stuff to head homeward, but stopped off in New York to say hello to Dr. Harry March, who was something of a general manager of the Giants for Mr. Mara. He was a bright-eyed, white-haired physician with a single, incurable phobia: "Postgraduate football," which was his term for the pros.

Dr. March had good news for me. Bob Folwell, the New York coach, was shorthanded for a game the Giants had booked in Palm Beach, Florida, for New Year's Day, and I was welcome to ship along, as an end. I said yes, packed my shoes, and went along. We got off the train in Palm Beach in the morning and played that afternoon.

The next fall, when I reported to Kansas City, Andrews took me aside. He said: "Steve, you are now a New York Football Giant. I have sold you to Tim Mara for $500."

He was right well pleased about the deal, because the price was staggering for those times, although I had seen fat hogs bring more in Kansas City.

I said I wouldn't report unless I was cut in for a share of the $500. He told me how hard up he was, but he didn't have to say much, because I was going to New York if I had to walk there.

I felt important, being sold to New York for a big price. Besides, I had been boosted up to $75 with the Cowboys, and, for all anybody knew, I might have the ante raised away up to $100 with the Giants.

Money wasn't even the main idea to me at that time. I loved to play football so much and whack the other fellows, that I guess they could have shaded me ten or fifteen dollars and I wouldn't have steamed up. I don't know why. It was simply living in a world that brought a lot of fun and contentment.

A fellow who played tackle opposite me in one of my final games as a Cowboy—and not the weekly pay check—paid me my finest compliment.

He was an ornery customer who gave me a time to break him down. He never stopped roughing it up, and he came back for more after I gave him a few good belts. I finally figured I had him sized up and told the quarterback to roll a certain play my way. I got the angle on him I expected, and let him have it. When the parade had marched over him he got up, with some of that fighting glint lost from his eyes, and said: "Owen, the trouble with you is you're not mean—you're just plain ugly."

4

THE HARDEST GAME I EVER PLAYED, AND THE ONE WHICH
took more out of me than any other, was the 13–7 win over
the Chicago Bears for the league title in 1927. We Giants
had to stop Bronko Nagurski, the great fullback. Tackling
him was like hitting an iron post. We also had to corner
Red Grange, one of the shiftiest halfbacks of all time.
Holding him was like tailing onto a greased pig.

I played that sixty minutes at tackle opposed to Jim
McMillen, later a world's championship wrestler. When
the gun ended the exhausting game both of us just sat
on the ground. He smiled in a tired way, reached over to
me, and we shook hands. We didn't say a word; we
couldn't. It was fully five minutes before we got up to go
to the dressing room.

That '27 world championship team of Giants was an
outstanding club of the Iron Man era of football, and it
ranks at least equal with any of the times. We won eleven
games, lost one, and tied one, and scored 172 points. We
allowed only 20 points in thirteen games, a league record
which has never been approached and never will be.

Our 1927 champions had one of Walter Camp's prize
selections, the celebrated Century Milstead, of Yale, at
tackle, opposite me. I would like to name the other fellows, to show what an effort Mr. Mara made to obtain a

representative national lineup in those early times. Here they are: Chuck Corgan, of Arkansas; Heck Garvey, of Notre Dame; Joe Guyon, of Carlisle and Georgia Tech; Jack Hagerty and George Murtaugh, of Georgetown; Hinkey Haines, of Penn State; Cal Hubbard, of Geneva (Pa.) College; Tut Imlay, of California; Paul Jappe and Jack McBride, of Syracuse; Jim Kendrick and Mule Wilson, of Texas A. & M.; Babe Parnell, of Colgate; Phil White, of Oklahoma; Doug Wyckoff, of Georgia Tech; Earl Potteiger, of Ursinus; and Al Nesser and Dick Stahlman, of the College of Hard Knocks.

Now that I've built up the '27 champions, whom I captained, I want to say they wouldn't stand a chance on a football field today against any club in the league. Not with the type of game we played. We were pretty much a smash and shove gang. We were bonecrackers. We were as good on the ground as the clubs of today, but we did not have speed and probably did not have the pass defense to check an attack of the modern era.

In football, at least, no matter what Ty Cobb says about baseball old-timers, the teams of my playing days could not compare with the sparkling, exciting, streamlined outfits the fans see now, which combine long-scoring ability, hitting power, over-all speed, highly developed tactics on offense and defense, and superb conditioning.

To make our 1927 gang of busters the equal of the Giants of today we would have had to drop the slow men, however rugged they were, take on half as many more men to put our squad to thirty, at least. Then we'd have had to get in better shape, and learn a new game, in which speed, science, and specialization would be added to the comparatively crude blasting power we had.

Take an outstanding tackle of the Iron Man age, Link Lyman of the Bears. He could not possibly play sixty minutes game after game in today's football. He wouldn't have a chance, for instance, against Arnie Weinmeister on defense, and Tex Coulter on offense, at tackle on the Giants. Obviously, he wouldn't, playing against two men in the platoon system. With platoons today we can maintain speed and stamina for sixty minutes, while in my time the same men worked until exhausted, with the pace of the game gradually slowing.

To make it personal, I know I could not hold off a Weinmeister–Coulter team, not for sixty minutes, and I was fast enough, big enough, and in good enough condition to be selected for a number of the "all-time" teams of early days.

Amazing changes have occurred in football in the short span of twenty years, so that it is a much better and an almost brand-new game, always providing you remember a player has to be just as willing to take the contact, and give it back, as we were back in those dark ages.

The main reason, of course, has to be in the rules. Year by year the trend has been to favor the offense. There have been few rules made to help the defense. The defense has had to rely on ingenuity to meet the challenge of rules which made possible a wider variety of attacking plays, by putting the ball in play at least twenty yards from the side line, by permitting a forward pass anywhere behind the line of scrimmage, by allowing a team four incomplete passes into the end zone before losing the ball. Those are just a few outstanding changes to boost offensive strength. In my day the ball was in play wherever downed, even one foot from the side line, which generally called for the waste of a down to move it inward. Our passer had to be five yards behind the line. We lost the ball on any incomplete pass into the end zone, even on first down.

Above all, we could not have tried the two-platoon

system, had we desired, because our substitution rule permitted a man to play only one time in each half. And, without question, teams nowadays practice more than we used to. They go to camp earlier and are in better shape squadwise.

The rules changes have made a more exciting and more difficult game of football. However, despite the advantages given the offense, balanced football and the prospect of a close and even low-scoring game between well-matched opponents exist as they did twenty-five years ago.

When you have a contest they don't run wild, regardless of the rules. It's just like two good pitchers settling down to a duel in baseball. They make the fans—and the hitters—forget the lively ball. Let's look over a number of scores in showdown games between good teams in recent years.

We might start with the great Chicago Bears team and its spectacular win over Washington for the title in 1940 by 73–0. But in the next decade see how the close ones came up more often than the attacking runaways in the title games. In '41 the same great Bears defeated New York 37–9, but they lost to Washington 14–6 in '42. They were back again in '43 to knock over Washington by 41–21. In '44 Green Bay defeated the Giants 14–7. Cleveland just nipped Washington, 15–14, in '45. The Bears beat the Giants 24–14 in '46. The Chicago Cardinals defeated Philadelphia 28–21 in '47, and in the following year Philadelphia got even with a 7–0 win, and went on for another season with a 14–0 decision over Los Angeles. In '50 Cleveland defeated New York 8–3 in a Conference play-off and defeated Los Angeles by 30–28.

I guess our Giant series with the Cleveland Browns is an even more pertinent illustration. When the high-scoring Browns came from the All-America Conference to the

NFL in 1950, their games with the Giants were the highlights of the season. We beat them 6–0 and 17–14.

In 1951 they won 14–13 and 10–0. Those were old-fashioned scores, but rules can't make scoring easier when opponents are in a balance. The big point to me is the tremendous increase in suspense for the fans—and the coaches—nowadays, because everyone realizes that one slip from perfection is likely to cost a touchdown, thanks to those easy-scoring rules.

Therefore, a low-score game nowadays is much more of a feat in over-all squad quality, intensity of training, and physical and mental teamwork than it was for our champions of '27.

One thing hasn't changed, however. That's the way humans think, and the fellow who could pull a surprise in my time was rewarded just as the sharp-minded quarterback is today. In our '27 title game, for instance, Henry L. (Hinkey) Haines called one of the smartest plays I have ever seen, to win for us. He stage-managed it perfectly.

The Bears had plodded downfield to our one-yard line, where we held 'em. Haines signaled for punt formation. The Bears dropped two men back to mid-field and jammed nine on the line.

We called signals in the open in those days, and Haines yelled to Mule Wilson, our punter, to be careful not to step beyond the end line for a safety. He asked that a towel be brought out to wipe the ball, because there was a patch of mud here and there on the field.

Haines completely fooled the Bears. When the ball was snapped he had dropped back a few yards to receive it. He threw over the line to Chuck Corgan, end, who used to play second base for the Dodgers, and Chuck went to the Bears' forty-yard line to start us toward a touchdown. Haines had set up the play beautifully, and not a man on our squad tipped it off. No better is seen today in the matter of surprise.

While we are comparing the old times with the new I must insist the attitude of the athlete hasn't changed a bit in eagerness to work. You can forget the moans we hear now and then about the passing of the Iron Men.

The good player today—the poor one doesn't stay long —wants to be in there whenever he thinks he can do you some good. He will stay in there for you when he is hurt, too, and resent it when he is taken out.

Ward Cuff, the great wingback of the Giants, was the equal of any Iron Man I ever saw for taking punishment. Sometimes when Cuff played he would be bandaged in so many places, to hold minor sprains together and protect bruises, that he looked like a mummy before he put on his uniform. It took us a couple of years to discover the tip-off when Cuff had been hurt. He was cool and impassive on the whole. When he suffered an injury, he would invariably laugh as the trainer or I asked him about his condition, and generally say: "Why, it doesn't amount to anything."

Al DeRogatis, our great defensive tackle who teamed with Weinmeister, is a wonder at hiding injuries, and I believe he displayed as much fortitude in several games as any boy I've ever seen. If I tried to save him, he would show me his feelings were deeply hurt, and when I kept him on the bench for what he considered too long a spell, he would actually insist strongly that he should go in.

I had to respect that spirit. I'd let DeRogatis play as long as I felt sure his condition was not bothering our defense. In trying to save his feelings once, I crossed up my own upstairs observer and phone man, Jim Lee Howell.

As the game began, I noticed that DeRogatis was not

starting to his outside to cover as fast as he should. I took him out, and he had to confess he had a muscle pull which broke him down on the outside. That was that, so far as I was concerned. "DeRo" was out of the game.

I had another guess coming. Al followed me, pleading to be sent back because there was nothing wrong with him to the *inside,* and he could cover there. I agreed, if Jon Baker, our middle lineman, thought he could get around fast enough to cover outside. He thought he could.

On the next defensive play, Howell frantically phoned that everything was going haywire. Baker was leaving his position, and DeRogatis was failing to cover. We had to explain to Jim that we were doing the best we could, because we had a player too tough to quit when he was hurt.

Tuffy Leemans, one of the most elusive runners of football history, was another who seemed to travel faster and harder when he had something wrong with him, and I could go on naming dozens. The human breed is the same; only the rules have changed.

Some of the old-timers may have been more colorful characters than our boys today, but on the whole they weren't any tougher. One of the most picturesque fellows we ever had on the Giants was Al Nesser of the famous Nesser brothers from Ohio. Al was big, and a terrific player, but never wore shoulder pads or helmet. I must mention he was partly bald and what hair he had was thin, to lead into the story.

Al played that entire roughhouse game for the title against the Bears in '27. That night a group of the players were talking it over in my room when Nesser stuck his head in the door. He bent over, and I never saw so many cuts, scratches, and bruises as he had on that bald head. He let the boys look it over, then quipped: "Which one of you guys told me the Bears couldn't hurt my head?"

But many a time there was no eagerness for punishment among our Iron Men. We played the Green Bay Packers in a day when they had great linemen, and the fabulous 270-pound Cal Hubbard, now an American League baseball umpire, backing up the middle. Even if our runners got through the line, gigantic Hubbard would knock the stuffing out of them. He was fast and hit like a sledge hammer. We quick-kicked on 'em all day, and after we scored a field goal for a 3–0 lead, nobody in our backfield wanted to carry the ball.

Harry Newman, our smallest back, at five-nine and 180 pounds, was quarterback. The others told him if he wanted to call running plays he could go ahead and run the ball. Newman had to rush if he wanted to have any chance to set up passes, and he became our whole attack. He passed to Dale Burnett for a touchdown, and we won 10–7. But not before little Newman had carried the ball thirty-nine times, a game record which still stands.

In the backfield that day we had a number of large men who decided they had enough, and one small chap with the gumption to keep plugging. That happens nowadays too, but we have more chance to eliminate the boys who want the other fellow to do it, because we have larger squads and more selectivity in personnel to begin with.

Hubbard was one of the most feared tackles in the game, and we were delighted when he came back to the Giants. Cal had played with us in 1927–28, and then had gone on to Green Bay, returning to New York in 1934. However, he hadn't yet finished damaging us Giants. When time was out during one game, I was standing behind him. He swung around and smashed his elbow accidentally into my face. I felt as though I'd been slugged with an axe, and I saw red. I must have thought Hubbard was still on the other side, because I yelled: "Watch those elbows—it's bad enough having to get hit with 'em in a game!"

The football of the late twenties seems old-fashioned now, but when I came up from Kansas City to New York it represented the best football of the times, and it made me feel that maybe I hadn't absorbed all there was to know about the game.

I had been a country boy trying to bust into the lineup at Kansas City, and I was in the same position with the Giants. I was the little boy from Phillips U. among all the big names from eastern colleges on the Giants' roster. I was a little fish in a big pool. The Giants had among their well-known college football heroes Arthur Carney, of Navy, Jack Hagerty, of Georgetown, Joe Alexander and Jack McBride, of Syracuse, and the great Haines, of Penn State.

It was a struggle for me to become a regular, but the fact that I was a country boy got me off to a good start. I reported to the Giants at Lake Ariel, Pennsylvania, on a Wednesday, and they had an exhibition scheduled for the following Sunday in Trenton, New Jersey. Clubs spent little time in camp in those years.

Alexander was the coach at the start of the season, but Joe, who is now an eminent heart specialist, was trying to practice medicine and play and coach, and he had to give up one or another of those jobs. He delegated much of the coaching to Earl Potteiger, who continued as head coach through 1927 and 1928.

Alexander started me in the Trenton exhibition, probably to have a look at me. The stars of the team put me through quite a bit of good-natured ribbing before the game. Though I took it well enough, I didn't like it, because I had an idea how to play the game too.

Whether I could play it or not, I had the laugh on my

teammates. They weren't in condition as yet, while I had never been out of shape, what with wrestling and such back in Oklahoma. It was a very hot day, and long before the end of the game they were almost falling over and asking for relief. I was able to work the full sixty minutes.

We can use our tongues pretty good out Oklahoma way when we get the chance, and they all began to lay off me when I continually inquired whether a fellow up here in New York played football for thirty, or forty, or fifty minutes, and not sixty minutes.

I played a lot of football in '26, and I was flying high with pride when Potteiger and Dr. Harry March made me captain for '27. For a fellow who had come in unknown to anybody—coaches, players, writers, or fans—only a year before, I considered that captaincy quite an honor.

The pioneering Dr. March ran the club for Mr. Mara, in an office of an apartment at Broadway and One hundred and third Street. All the players moved in on him from time to time, and the feature of the whole layout was a big check book on the Doc's desk. It was always available to team members who needed advances on their pay. We kept Doc busy writing. But he enjoyed it, and great in all ways was his contribution to the success of professional football in New York City during those early days.

Mr. Mara left the club almost entirely to the Doc, because he had many other interests, and football amounted to a hobby, and an expensive one in those days when you couldn't give tickets away for some games. Mr. Mara always had a great sense of humor, and more than once he has told me that he founded the Giants in 1925 "on brute strength and ignorance." Meaning the players provided the strength and he the ignorance.

No coach could have had a more understanding owner than Mr. Mara. He always had a fine sense of the delicate balance between a front office and the management of the team in action. He steadfastly refrained from a practice which has wrecked more than one team, in his appreciation that the front office could not fairly, nor with good effect, interfere with the coach in decisions of strategy or use of personnel. And you can bet I never tried to push my nose into the front office.

This fine sensibility about football has been maintained by his sons, John V. Mara, now president, and Wellington Mara, now secretary-treasurer. I have worked as coach for the Maras since 1931 without a contract or paper of any kind. The understanding has been that if either party wasn't happy the deal was off with mutual good will. That's the only way to operate. But you have to find the right people before trying it.

I recall one of the few times Mr. Mara was on our bench during a game. It was the 3–0 win we scored over the Bears in 1933. After the game the winning team is entitled to the football, but in those days we sometimes had to wrestle for it. As the game ended I spotted red-haired (then) Mr. Mara out in the mud over his shoe tops tackling a big Bear for the ball. We helped him get it. As he scraped the mud off his shoes in the dressing room he grinned and said: "I'm sure a smart Irishman. I give away fifty or sixty of those things every year, but I'm out on the field wrestling some big guy for a football."

A fellow can certainly see the country if he plays football. I had been all through the Midwest with the Cowboys. I went to Florida after the '25 season as a Giant reserve. When the '27 season ended I signed on with C.C. (Cash-and-Carry) Pyle to play eight games in California on a squad headed by Red Grange. Never did I suspect how much more of the country I was to see under the guidance of Pyle, one of the most ingenious and imaginative promoters of all time. This fellow was to lead me into every city, village, and farm through a good part of the nation, on his fantastic "bunion derbies."

By the time we ended the Grange tour in the middle of February in '28, Pyle had arranged to run a foot-race marathon from Los Angeles to New York. He offered huge prizes, with the expectation of getting back the money, and more, by collecting various sums from cities his troupe visited.

He talked several of the players, Owen among them, into going along as patrol judges, starters, and checkers. He had entries from three hundred runners, representing all parts of this country and many sections of Europe, with one lone hopeful from Rhodesia, South Africa. Pyle had arranged for a huge Army field kitchen and cook tent to roll along with us to feed the racers and hands.

I got to be a starter, and would borrow a pistol from the local sheriff or constable to get going every morning at 4 or 5 A.M. The patrol judges would be spotted along the course to see no one hitched a ride. The marathon went twenty to seventy-five miles a day and took about eighty days. It probably attracted as much attention and newspaper space as anything that ever happened. Thousands lined the highways wherever we went, but the same thousands didn't come into the parks where they had to pay to see the end of the daily runs. Hardly anybody paid. Public indifference was frightful.

Our first trouble came with the cooks. After they had struggled through the desert for a couple of weeks and reached New Mexico, they cried "Enough!" and jumped camp. We nominated Ralph Scott, who had played football for Wisconsin and for the Bears, to run the cooking. Scott put whatever he could lay his hands on into huge kettles, boiled it up, and fed the lot. He called it Mulligan stew the first day, and seemed to like the name, because he never claimed to have cooked anything else while he was chef. When we got to more populous areas and big cities, we ate at restaurants whenever Pyle had enough money. However, money got scarcer and scarcer, and Pyle, who could talk almost anybody into anything, induced others to help him out financially. We finally finished with seventy runners competing in a twenty-four-hour race at Madison Square Garden, New York City.

The cross-country derby was a great experience for me, because it showed me what the human body could stand in athletics. I saw many of those fellows with shin splints so bad they could hardly step down the road at dawn. But by 10 A.M., when the sun had warmed them up, they could run fast. I never saw fellows who hated to get out of anything as much as those who finally broke down along the way and had to withdraw, crippled, nauseous, and helpless.

The marathon was won by Andy Payne, an Oklahoma Indian boy. (Wouldn't you know?) He had never run before competitively and didn't afterward. His style won for him. He was opposed by many famous Swedish and Finnish long-distance runners, who started out as if they were going to hide from the rest. But they had the conventional high stride, and the continual pounding they took in that fashion caused them to come down with blisters and shin splints.

Payne, to the contrary, only shuffled along and never pounded his feet or legs. He never went fast, but never stopped. He won the $25,000 first prize, and gave up running. He had made his stake in short order, and went back to Oklahoma to become a clerk in a state court.

Pyle would not give up his marathon idea. If it wouldn't work from west to east, he decided it had to go from east to west, and I went with him in the spring of '29 on a New York–Los Angeles deal.

He organized the marathon in style. In fact, for weeks he had people waiting outside the door of his suite in the Hotel Astor to be sold this or that. Pyle had lined up a variety show, with comedians, a chorus, a girls' band, and a tent which seemed bigger to me than any I had ever seen Barnum and Bailey use. The first time his crew tried to put up the tent in Philadelphia, they didn't make it until 10 P.M., after the customers had left. A windstorm in Maryland blew the tent to bits, and Pyle had to arrange for theater bookings thereafter.

But we started luxuriously. C.C. had a dozen Chevrolet autos painted fire-engine red, and a big bus fitted out like a Pullman car with a small kitchen installed.

Trouble was he forgot to pay for the cars, and sheriffs picked 'em up along the way until we ran out of Chevvies at Cumberland, Maryland. By the time we reached Columbus, Ohio, the sheriff caught up with his bus.

The whole outfit was on its feet then, but we managed to take that cavalcade of courage and credit across country without transportation, excepting for auto agencies that might oblige with cars from hop to hop for the publicity value to them.

We reached the stage when we had no money to pay the actors or anybody. We depended on a share-and-share alike whackup of the show's receipts after each performance. At one town the total receipts amounted to three dollars.

For some reason we struck it rich in Durant, Oklahoma, near the Texas border, with a terrific crowd, but after the curtain went up, Pyle learned that half the company had been delayed by floods and wasn't on hand. The big Red

River and a flock of tributaries were on a rampage. But so was the paying public.

The crowd got to muttering, but we had to pacify 'em or go hungry. Pyle sent an acrobat out front with an athletic trainer and a marathon runner, to do handstands and tumbles and such. When they almost tore the scenery apart the act was so funny it seemed rehearsed. But when five-minute comedians tried to spiel for half an hour, the roar of the crowd began to rise, and we started to wonder whether we could get safely down an alley with the money.

Just at that critical point the rest of the troupe arrived. The crowd went home happy, and we didn't have to leave hungry. We got twenty-five bucks apiece, a godsend.

Part of the field of finishers got their prize money, part didn't. The bedraggled company arrived at Los Angeles and drew no more attention than in New York a year before. Johnny Salo, of Passaic, New Jersey, won and was paid. He returned to Passaic to join the police force and later was killed at a sandlot baseball game when the ball hit him in the head while he was trying to push back the crowd. For three thousand miles on foot across the country he had dodged cars and trucks, only to meet his end at a peaceful baseball game in his own home town.

One time on the trip west Pyle was very short of cash and didn't have enough to get the company out of the hotel. He asked me if I could lend him $150. I thought that over a minute or two. I had a few dollars in the bank from the football season, but I didn't want to buy a share of that marathon. On the other hand, I believe in obliging a fellow if possible, so I went down to the manager and asked him to cash a check.

He hemmed and hawed a while, and said he would if Mr. Pyle would okay it. He phoned up to Pyle and got the approval he wanted.

When I returned to the room I never saw a man get such a laugh out of anything in my life. It couldn't have been much funnier, at that. Pyle didn't have a quarter, you might say, but he could okay my check to bail himself out.

Pyle promised to return the money soon, but as the days went on I had a hunch he'd forgotten all about it, and I decided to help myself. As soon as we reached the next town I rushed to the bank to pick up the money he had been guaranteed for showing there. It happened to be $150. He learned later, of course, that I had claimed the money, and he asked for it.

"You owe me this money," I said. "I'm keeping it."

He argued, but lost.

Finally he grinned, and asked: "Okay, but will you give me two dollars to eat on?"

I did.

On the whole Pyle was a great boss. He treated everybody well when he made it, and we didn't mind going short when he didn't. As a promoter he had an idea a minute, and maybe that was his trouble. He had so many he didn't ever get to carrying any through to a proper finish. I don't know how many stunts he tried to put over while I was associated with him. One of the amusing by-products of his "bunion derbies" was C.C. Pyle's Patent Foot Box, for three thousand maladies of the human foot.

Despite his misfortunes with the cross-country marathons, Pyle refused to give up the idea. He simply made it grander and more spectacular. What he proposed, but never could get off, was a dance marathon from the City Hall in New York to the Arc de Triomphe in Paris. He ballyhooed it as the "World's Greatest Experiment in Chiropody." Other people didn't think so, and he couldn't raise the cash required.

Pyle had been one of the first to make radio transcripts. He did a terrific publicity job with Red Grange, when the latter came out of Illinois as the most celebrated football player of his era. Through the contacts the energetic Pyle made for him, Grange must have taken several thousand dollars from football and its side products. Pyle even started a rival professional football league! That also flopped.

I had the pleasure of rooming with Red on the marathons. I had the respect for him one must grant to one of the great players of all time. He rated high in football, not only for running, but also for blocking and defensive skill, as taught to him by Bob Zuppke. Grange is a player who comes along once in a lifetime.

Pyle spent some of Red's money when times were bad, but no one ever heard Grange say an unkind word about Charlie. He had the utmost faith in Cash-and-Carry, and admiration for him. I respected Red the more for his manly and loyal attitude toward Pyle, an unfortunate dreamer.

The success of the Grange football tours, beginning in 1925, led many to form an illusion about pro football and its cash value. Grange, for instance, drew 64,300 to the Polo Grounds on his first professional appearance in New York in December, 1925. That's all the gatekeepers counted. Mr. Mara estimates there were more than 70,000 in the park, considering that thousands didn't bother to pay but stormed gates and scaled fences. That was the most spectacular turnout in New York football history, but it was just that—a one-time spectacle.

Two years later the Giants played in the same park in the rain to eighty cash customers, and we were the champion team of the year.

But Grange gave the game its first press clippings and

widespread public notice. Toward the end of the decade there were more signs that it was going to grow out of infancy into a pretty husky child. The growth was to be slow, very slow, and immeasurable fortunes, which could never be regained, were to be spent in its support before it attained its major stature of today.

Football made its first move to capture the public when it began to open up going into the thirties. Bennie Friedman, the great passer from Michigan, was one of those most responsible. He played for Detroit under my former boss at Kansas City, LeRoy Andrews. Mr. Mara tried to buy Friedman, and, when he failed, he bought out Andrews and most of the Detroit club, to get Friedman. Andrews came here for 1929, and the Giants for the first time began to get away from the smash-and-shove game of the Iron Men.

In a few years, for instance, the game definitely grew more exciting. In 1933 we played two games with the Bears which illustrated both forms of play, the old and the new. In the first game, we won 3–0, when Ken Strong kicked a field goal three times. One field goal, that is. He made it from the fifteen—offside. He made it from the twenty—offside. It counted from the twenty-five.

My brother Bill was playing guard on those field goal attempts opposite Walter Kopcha of the Bears, who is now a noted physician. Kopcha repeated each time Strong kicked: "Please, Lord, don't let that ball go through." I noticed Bill didn't block him to speak of, and asked why after the game.

Bill bristled: "What do you mean—you think I would hit a man when he's praying?"

We lost to the Bears for the title that year, 23–21, in a game crammed with excitement and surprises. The lead changed seven times, and, as the final gun sounded, an official near our bench asked: "Who won?"

That was the game in which we made our center, Mel Hein eligible to receive a forward pass. He was on the end of the line. He snapped the ball to Newman, and Harry stepped up to pass it back to Hein between the latter's legs. Hein walked thirty yards before Carl Brumbaugh of the Bears got suspicious and tackled him on the five-yard line.

On the last play of the game we tried a planned lateral surprise, which would have worked excepting for Grange's quick thinking. Red Badgro made a nifty catch of a forward, and was to lateral to Dale Burnett, who was in the clear. Grange coming up fast with the field in view, spotted Burnett and tackled Badgro around the arms to prevent the trick. That game, with its stratagems and excitement, and its widespread publicity, helped arouse the public to the entertainment value of football.

That new style of open, passing game, which proved so popular, came to stay when Friedman arrived from Detroit. We had an edge on most clubs with Bennie, one of the early great passers, on our side, and we won twelve, lost one, and tied one in '29, and had a thirteen-won, four-lost record in '30. In the next season, however, Andrews may have pushed his luck too far with Mr. Mara. He was a wonderful fellow, with a great deal of go about him, but we got the idea he wanted to dip into matters which weren't exactly his business.

Whatever it was, the whole operation did not do well in '31, when we split twelve games and tied one, and Andrews resigned with two games to go. Friedman and I acted as co-coaches. In this role I thought back to the pleasure of meeting the fabulous Knute Rockne the previous year. The celebrated Notre Dame coach had brought the Four Horsemen and an All-Star team to New York to play the Giants for Mayor Walker's fund for the unemployed. Incidentally, the fund received $115,000 from the game.

The All-Stars came to the Polo Grounds to work out the day before the game, and I introduced myself to Rockne. He tried to kid me a little.

"Oh, sure, one of the Owen boys," he said, with reference to brother Bill. "There's two of you and both of you are very, very tough to play. Don't know what we'll do tomorrow."

Several of his players, whom I knew, already had told me Rockne felt sure he could win.

I answered: "Don't know about that. We will be glad to do anything to help you today, but tomorrow what we do won't be to your advantage."

The Giants won, and it was the last game Rockne coached. He died shortly after, in an airplane crash in a Kansas cornfield, March, 1931. I had thought a whole lot about this football genius through that winter, and I wondered if his equal would ever be seen again. It hasn't.

Rockne is an apt figure at this place in my story, as the more open kind of football begins its unchecked march to popular acclaim. He, with Gus Dorais, practically gave birth to the forward pass, as a Notre Dame player against Army in 1920. Also, he was the inspirational type of coach who captivated the public with word and act.

Rockne had such a dynamic personality that he inspired the other fellows to beat him, maybe fully as much as he inspired his own men to win. He was a perpetual challenge to the other team throughout his career.

Men of Rockne's qualities make sports. That inspirational leadership glamorizes the game for the general public. I always felt sports had a tremendous boost in the

twenties toward present popularity because there was
Rockne in football and John McGraw in baseball. The
latter was of the same vibrant temperament as Rockne. I
was pretty close to his methods and his manners because
I worked at the Polo Grounds for Jim Tierney, the Giants'
baseball secretary, for several summers.

After the 1931 season, I went to work for Mr. Mara in
his coalyard on the Harlem River. Needing a new coach
for '32, he often asked my opinion on various prospects,
which he listed and discussed. My nominee from the start
was Guy Chamberlain, a great end at Nebraska, and a
superman in the pros at Canton and at Cleveland. He
always could beat you one way or another, and he proved
himself a dynamic leader as coach of the Frankford Yellow
Jackets. As the name of this fellow and that came up, I
stood firm for Chamberlain. I pulled for him because I
wanted to play under him.

One day Mr. Mara phoned me: "We've decided on a
coach for the Giants."

I answered: "Fine, who is it?"

Mr. Mara said: "I'm tired of buying uniforms for you,
Owen. You're the coach."

He hung up. I nearly dropped the phone. I had to think
it over. I didn't want to quit playing. I called back.

"What about Chamberlain?" I inquired.

"I've made up my mind on the coach," Mr. Mara
snapped, "and it's going to be you."

He hung up again. That was final. I was the coach.

5

~~~~~~~~~~

THERE MUST BE THOUSANDS OF GOOD FOOTBALL COACHES IN the country, or even in New York alone. That's what I would judge from my mail. Countless fans have told me exactly how to run the Giants through the years, in the firm conviction, I assume, that they know more about it than I do.

Maybe they do know more. Maybe they are better coaches. But I am one of the lucky fans who wanted to be a coach and who wound up with the job. I appreciate the interest of the thousands of other coaches who didn't make it, but I can't go thousands of ways at once. I can only go my way, right or wrong.

In the course of twenty years of coaching I have come to several conclusions. Summed up, coaching is a matter of fundamentals, the hardest kind of work, and an understanding of human relations.

Good common sense in trying to understand and handle the boys who come to him is the most important and most difficult part of the coach's job. He might as well throw away his play book if he can't get along with the team and bring out the highest expression of team play among the fellows.

To put it another way, coaching is not primarily technical; it is human first of all.

We have all heard that coaches are supposed to build character.

My idea is to build confidence, and character will come.

Few boys graduating from college have the experience or the maturity to support self-confidence. Almost any boy is looking for guidance, and most of them need it. The football coach must see that they get it.

Until a coach is able to make the boys believe in themselves, and in him, and then rely on one another in team play, he isn't going to get far, no matter what kind of material he may have.

That idea of self-reliance reminds me of the time I was a high-school principal back in Oklahoma.

After the football season with the Cowboys in 1924, I thought it was about time to draw dividends from the years I had put into schooling. Armed with a certificate entitling me to teach in the grade and high schools of my state, I stopped in on Dr. McCash, president of Phillips U., and asked him whether he could help me to a job.

Could he? He acted as if he knew I was coming in. He sat me down while he called the state superintendent of schools and told him he had just the man for the job at Binger.

Then he turned to me: "Steve, you are going to be the high-school principal at Binger. Congratulations."

Well, principals' jobs don't grow on cottonwoods for anybody passing along the road, and I wanted to know why the job was open. Dr. McCash cleared his throat and explained: "Oh, they had a little trouble down there. The last principal was knifed by one of the students."

I started to get up, never having been a fellow to look for trouble, but he stopped me.

"Steve," he said, kind of pleading, "you are just the man for the job. I know you can handle the teaching end of it, history and math, and I am sure, with your experience, you will keep order. I know those boys are a rough lot, but they are not bad boys, Steve. They will take to you."

I didn't know what I was getting into, but I went down to Binger, a town of five hundred, with eighty kids and six teachers in the high school. Naturally, I inquired right off about the boy who had knifed the principal. The teachers and the sheriff agreed the boy was just a little hot-tempered, and hadn't cut the principal much, just enough to drive him out of town. One teacher said the boy had scratched the principal a little, and the latter lost his nerve.

The boy who used the knife was a husky fellow off a farm who weighed about 225. He looked like many a guard I had been playing with that fall. I made a point to catch up with him. He came around the end of the schoolhouse one day in my first week, taking a chaw out of a big plug of tobacco.

"Don't you know you can't do that around here," I said to him. "Give me that plug."

The tobacco lasted me a week.

I began talking to that boy, and found out he was a little slow grasping things. The other fellows nagged him and picked on him because of his lack of mental speed. Nothing crueler than kids when they have a mind to be.

But you know, those boys didn't have any athletic equipment at all, which was a serious handicap in promoting any kind of morale.

I did the best I could by thinking up a game the boys called Black Man, for some reason or other. We had two sides lining up facing each other, and close together, as in football. The idea was for both sides to charge hard and fast to see which one would be first to get a fellow through the rough-and-tumble.

I played in that game opposite the boy who used the knife. I knew far too many tricks for him, but he began to catch on and brightened up considerably. He took an interest in the school from then on, lost his surliness, and I found him a fine companion when I took him out hunting several times.

All that boy needed was a slap on his broad back. He didn't have much of an opportunity or as much talent as the other boys, but I got the best out of him by using the same human principles that I had learned from my folks and my coaches. He turned out all right after he got his self-confidence.

It works the same in football, from the coach's point of view. Ed Danowski was one of the finest passers the Giants ever had, and one of the most accurate in football history. I believe he still holds the record for fewest interceptions over a long period.

But he was not a passer at Fordham, and when he became our Number One man he didn't have that backlog of confidence to make him play up to his full capabilities. He wasn't sure. He didn't have faith in forward passing, much less in himself.

I bet him an ice cream soda one day that I could think up a pass play which would go for a touchdown—sure pop —if he would call it and do his job with assurance when it came up. That was a risky bet. I had to wait for the spot, but I managed to dream up a new play. Danowski was to fake a forward, then throw laterally to Andy Marefos out on the flank. Marefos, a good passer, was to wing one downfield to Vince Dennery, end. When I called it, it worked. Dennery went sixty to score. Danowski beamed as if he had revolutionized the game of football. I made a big show, giving him full credit before the team, and Ed was sort of deadly on a throw forever after.

There is another general idea which goes along with character building, and that involves the pep talk. Many of the fans, and a great many viewers of our Giants' TV show, write to inquire what I tell the boys in the dressing room before the game. Some, I know, believe the coach has such command of elocution and rhetoric that he can inspire boys far above their talents.

So far as these pep talks go, I believe the less the coach says, the better. Ralph Hutchinson, one of our players about ten years back, told a story which, to my mind, includes the ideal pep talk.

Hutchinson played at Chattanooga for Scrappy Moore, a colorful character, successful coach, and great fellow. Moore had the habit of stomping around the dressing room before a game, kicking at everything in sight while he talked.

One day the boys decided to take care of Scrappy. They draped a couple of jerseys over a foot scale in the middle of the floor. Moore began to speak, kicked at those jerseys as hard as he could, and threw his knee out. He lay there on his back, bewildered, with the pep all drained out of him. But as the team filed out he simply had to yell: "Gang, go out there and fight 'em!"

That's far enough to go with a pep talk. I know it's easy for a coach to think he might be able to get boys fired up through a speech, but that's not the way to do it. Good team spirit is something that comes on gradually. When the coach has the boys believing in him and willing to do a job under orders for him, he doesn't need a pep talk.

A coach can tell whether a team is mentally alert for a game the minute he enters the dressing room.

If the boys are quiet, and tending to business, and getting taped and bandaged without kidding the trainer, the coach knows they are ready to play football. If the gang is laughing and having a big time, you know darn well they are not concentrating and that they may be in for a rough time. In that situation the coach may be able to change the attitude by putting a sharp word to individuals here and there, and giving the squad a stiff talk on plans and strategy—but not on pep.

A coach with a good team always has a sort of playing coach on the squad, a boy who is going to go all out every time and who is a respected leader among the rest of the fellows. I mean men such as Tuffy Leemans, Otto Schnellbacher, Dale Burnett, Arnie Weinmeister, Ward Cuff, Ray Flaherty, Jim Poole, to mention just a few of the take-charge men we have had on the Giants. There have been others, and every coach can name some from his past.

If the coach can get the word through to that key player, and convince him things are amiss, he can be sure the boy is going to eat out some of the fellows who are looking forward to a lark. By himself, he may be able to get the club ready for a fight. One of the great compensations in football coaching is to see one of these take-charge players stomp out indifference before a game. It makes the job worth while.

There is another angle to attitude. A coach also must be ready for a game, if he expects the team to get in the swing. The feeling of the coach is passed on, very sensitively, in all the contacts he has with his men from day to day. If he shows any doubt or uncertainty, you can bet it will be absorbed and exaggerated in the minds of the players.

Pep talks can do as much damage as good, I feel, because emotionalism can get a team so high it will not function properly. Remember those boys about to play are keyed up anyway. Adding to their nervous tension may make the strings snap completely and put them in a jittery, fumbling mood.

I was tempted to sound off at half time once in 1951, when our men trailed the Eagles by 17–0 in a game I figured they could win handily. But when I stepped into the dressing room I realized no speech by me was required. I could see those boys were so ashamed of themselves that my words, or even my presence, weren't necessary. They knew they could play better, just as well as I did.

So I went ahead just as if it were an even game. I went into the routine summary at half time, and set out the strategy for the second half. I merely closed with one needling line, an expressed hope they would look better than they had in the first half.

Those boys were the hottest team I ever saw, offensively and defensively, in the second half. The Eagles got the kickoff on their twenty, and in three plays our defense threw 'em for a safety. On the safety kick, Em Tunnell ran for a touchdown. The Eagles actually lost ground on attack in the second half, and our boys scored twenty-three points in the third period alone.

I have another story which illustrates why the coach is better off with his mouth closed at certain times when he wants to open it. This also depicts the highest type of team spirit.

At the Polo Grounds in 1950 we were playing the Browns an extremely hard and close game, and they led us 6–3 with a minute to go in the half. We had 50,000 fans cheering for us. The Browns had just kicked a field goal and kicked off to us. Jimmy Ostendarp, rookie halfback, forgot to cover the bounding ball, which was a free ball on a kickoff. A Cleveland player fell on it at our one-yard line. Otto Graham went over for a touchdown in a single play, and they led 13–3.

That was the worst kind of break a team could get. It was a blunder that wouldn't happen in ten seasons of pro ball, and probably not even in ten years of good high-school ball. I guess you would have to check it off to lapse of memory by Ostendarp, who had known better from the time he began playing the game. It shocked our fans, too, because they were "up" for this game.

What I worried about most was the effect on our team. Would a tough one like that break their spirit? Would they sulk over Jimmy's blunder? If so, what could I say to pull them together?

The answer came immediately. They showed me what a grand outfit they were as soon as the half ended. They swarmed over Ostendarp on the field, telling him to forget it, and that they were going to get it back for him. In the clubhouse a few seconds later, every man made a point of going over to that brokenhearted kid to give him a few encouraging words and a clap on the back, and I never heard one boy speak in censure of Jimmy that day or ever after.

I knew I wasn't needed in that atmosphere, and went about the locker room as quietly as I could to check up on technical points with my captains on offense and defense. Otherwise I didn't say a word.

The gang got it back for Jimmy. In the second half they pounded that rugged Cleveland line for two touchdowns and a 17–13 win. No matter how long Ostendarp lives, I don't think he will ever forget what a fine lot of stand-up teammates he had in 1950. I won't forget, because football doesn't have any stronger team spirit than our boys showed that day. It's something far above the yardstick of dollars and cents, victory and defeat.

If a coach has that knack of getting along with boys and understanding them to get the most out of them, there is no mystery to his job except material and hard work.

I often liken a coach to a monkey-on-a-stick. When he's going up, he's sure to see the other fellow coming down. And vice versa. Without adequate material, even Houdini couldn't win. And when two coaches have comparable material, the one who works hardest and has an intuitive feel for the attitude of his men will be the winner.

Many have criticized me for not playing more showy football, with more throwing and more tricks. That burns me up at times, but I will take any amount of it so long as I never lose sight of sound football. Some people forget a team still has to block and tackle well to win. It's a contact game, and not an aerial circus on the flying trapeze.

Some call me a defensive coach and sneer when they say it. Well, I'll take that, if you allow that the object of the game is to win. I would rather win by 3–0 than lose by 38–36. Defense is still half the game, and I like defense. As a coach, I would have to like it, because it has to work if I want to win. Ball games—baseball, too—between comparable teams are lost on mistakes, and if you have a mistake in your defense, a weakness or an erratic player, today's offense will murder you for it.

Exciting football which is also sound depends on the individual brilliance of the personnel more than on the coach's thinking and strategy, provided the proper timing has been achieved.

It is extremely difficult for a coach to think up a new variation of a basic play. Those who substitute variations just to be "new and different" invariably fail. The good ones don't try. They are going to depend on the fundamental winning plays, and not confuse a team with a flood of variations which are little or no better than the standard plays.

The winning coach is going to bet on his great passer, runner, or receiver to be a little better than the other side's. He will set store in fundamental football, in native traits of alertness and smartness, and in physical attributes of speed and power. A winning play, often the most dramatic incident of the game, is generally a standard play made exciting by the brilliance of the individual. Football is a game between men, and the player who is a little better than his opponent wins. The great player is one who is a little better than his game.

But fans like tricks, and that is very often a terrible temptation for a home coach to throw in a little flummery. The home fans see his team week after week. They know the style, and are tempted to say it's "the same old stuff," no matter how sound or how successful. On the other hand, the fans see a visiting team only once. They are looking at something new and are likely to marvel at the wonderful "deception" in the attack, especially if the visiting team wins.

But when he is back home that coach of the visiting team has his problems convincing the fans he has such marvelous "deception." They see his stuff week after week, too. When a coach has a chance to think it over, as I have had for more than twenty years, he can only decide to stick to winning football games the best way he knows.

There is another thought which goes along with fancy football. That's the idea of chance-taking, gambling on the field. Many fans want the coach to take more risks. Most often, that means they, without realizing it, want him to give the other side more chances to win.

I have always liked a good gamble, but it has to be a good one, with the odds about even on winning and losing.

I got away from the "house games" away back when I left the Texas oil fields. I will always let the other fellow take the bad gamble. If I am ahead of him, he might have to take it; if I am behind, I am going to do my best to avoid taking it and to find some other way. Gambling is bad football, unless you can see a 50–50 break.

Let's look at a couple of "gambles" the Giants have taken in key games against very formidable opponents. In 1943, when we were battling Washington for the eastern title, we had fourth down and needed three yards for a touchdown against them, with four minutes to go. We could have tied with a field goal, but I ordered a running play. Bill Paschal went off tackle for a touchdown, and we won.

In that 1950 Browns game, mentioned before in connection with Ostendarp, we had fourth down and three to go, with about five minutes remaining. A field goal would have tied, and, incidentally, hurt them more than it would have us, because we defeated them in our first meeting at Cleveland. But I called the running play. Joe Scott went off their tackle behind a block by Bill Swiacki, and we won.

Both plays were hailed as daring gambles. They were no such things to me. Those were good gambles. I was betting on my defense to hold the other side if we failed to make the touchdown. Then they would have to make a hurried kick from their end zone, we might have the chance for a run-back, and there would still be time for the field goal. Risky, of course, but with a reasonably sure tie in view, and not so chancy if you have faith in your men.

But I am not going to gamble on making a yard on fourth down in my territory unless that is all I have left in a desperate situation. If I did that often, the folks sure would say I am daring, and I would soon be looking for a job in the pickle works or back on the farm, but not in football.

In my early days as coach I had many a keen debate on tactics with George M. Cohan, the beloved entertainer of the American stage. He was an intense Giant baseball fan and kept his interest in Giants going along into football. Cohan was a shrewd student of both sports and was one of the sharpest observers of both that I have known. He seldom bothered with statistics but bore right to the heart of any game, to the single pitch which had won or lost, or the one block or pass or run which had been vital, even when it wasn't in a scoring play.

We often argued about calculated risks in football. In short, gambles. There was one which we never could settle, because it got down to a matter of splitting seconds. That was the "touchdown-rather-than-field-goal" example which I mentioned back a bit. He would point out that if I took my chance for the touchdown and lost, the defending team would surely give up two points for a safety in exchange for the right of a free kick from the twenty. Then I would be so far in my territory that I never would have the chance at a field goal.

In rebuttal I said I would take the handicap of added distance after a free kick, because they were giving me the privilege of winning, rather than tying with a field goal, when they took the safety.

He would concede that point, but I had to allow he was right, depending on how much time was left. And that's what it gets down to—the time showing on the clock when you get the ball for your last chance. If it is only a minute or so, the percentages are fairly heavy against you. With around two minutes remaining, I think the gamble has an odds-against chance, but one to think over. With three minutes to go, it begins to look attractive and rate about even-up.

Cohan was one of many show people attracted to the Giants. I have noticed through the years that many folks in show business and in sports seem to be drawn to each other. I guess that's because both are in very speculative lines of work, in which no one can be sure of a comfortable afternoon cutting 6 per cent coupons once a year.

Then, too, athletes and show people seem to have similar superstitions. John Cannady, Giant backer-up, not only carries a rabbit foot but talks to it from time to time. Many other players have good-luck charms. Players will refuse to have a sweat shirt laundered, no matter how awful it looks, because they are on a winning streak. They will insist on wearing the same socks game after game. Those things are taken for granted by players. They may laugh a little about it, but nobody wants to be the one to break another fellow's charm. An old pair of socks will lie around a clubhouse through the year if all concerned know that they represent somebody's luck and are not to be disturbed.

Many a fellow wears the same hat, or suit, or tie while on a good streak. I do too, but when I first became a coach I wore the same suit all the time, win or lose, because it was the only one I owned.

I always got a kick out of Greasy Neale, the great strategist of the Philadelphia Eagles, wearing a straw hat in a snowstorm. The season had changed on Greasy, but he couldn't give up his lucky hat until his side had run out of the hat's luck.

George Halas, owner and coach of the Chicago Bears, had a habit of throwing his hat on the ground and jumping on it. But one time he made the mistake of jumping on a brand-new, pretty, lemon-colored chapeau. That cured him of the practice.

Pete Cawthon, athletic director at Alabama and former coach of Texas Tech and of the professional Dodgers, used to tear up a cowboy hat every game. Just peel it to shreds. I imagine he did it unconsciously one winning day, and didn't dare give up the habit for fear of a jinx.

I guess my wife thought I was going off the trolley one day about ten years ago. I had married the unsuspecting Miriam Sweeny in 1935, and she may not have had grounds to understand her ghastly mistake until about five years later.

The easiest and normal way to leave our apartment in New York City is through the living-room door. But this day she looked in wonderment when I said good-by and then squeezed my two hundred and eighty pounds past a bed in the bedroom to leave by a rather inaccessible door.

To her mounting surprise, I did it day after day, until I sheepishly explained. I had gone out that door in a sort of absent-minded way one Sunday morning before a game, and we had won a real big one. Ever after I simply had to use that door to leave for the football field. If it worked once, it might work again.

Also, I always go to the Polo Grounds over the same route when we are going good, whether I drive or take a cab. Another of my "success" secrets now revealed for the first time: I never leave the football field without walking, if at all possible, between the goal posts.

Seriously, I don't know what part, if any, these superstitions play in football and in coaching. They do seem a grasping for something which a fellow can keep going for him in an insecure and risky business. Down deep, I guess we all need a little help from somewhere, even if it's only imaginary.

More often than not, it's that way down on the bench and on the field during a game time. Nothing is certain. The football is the boss. There is a tension which is difficult to describe, but which a coach often notes because players act in strange ways.

For instance, most players, great and small, have that nervous, "stage-fright" feeling before a game which they say many of the great actors cannot shake. One of the few who seemed to be without nerves was Ward Cuff. He was a cucumber, a pail of ice water. But one day he did get the jitters. Because of injuries, I had asked him to shift to safety on defense. On the bench he complained of being ill. We called the doctor in a hurry. The doctor could not find anything wrong. Finally he told Cuff: "That stomachache is just a bunch of butterflies down there. You have the jitters, and you'll be all right when play starts."

Cuff did work a great game at safety.

To the present time, Joe Stydahar, coach of the Los Angeles Rams, has such a nervous stomach that he generally throws up at game time. He did it habitually when he was a great tackle with the Chicago Bears, and he did it while his team was winning the world title in 1951. We played the Rams an exhibition in Little Rock, Arkansas, in 1950, and Jack Mara, our president, who had never believed the stories about Joe, went into his dressing room to exchange greetings. Sure enough, Joe was sick. Sometimes that upset feeling impairs a fellow's efficiency. Sometimes it settles him down for a good game.

The pressure comes out in different ways, depending on the player's temperament. I had a boy on the Giants about ten years ago, Jiggs Kline, from Emporia State Teachers College, who showed me a new one. Jiggs had been rapped in the head, and I took him out. Under no circumstances will a coach take a chance with a boy who has been hurt about the head until he has a definite clearance from the doctor, who is usually right on the bench.

But Jiggs couldn't understand that. He kept after me to go back in play until I made it clear he was through for the day. To show me what he thought of me he went to the bench and sat down facing the stands, with his back to me. He "fixed me" by staying that way through the game.

Fellows in that supercharged atmosphere of competition often find laughs in strange places. One day Tilly Manton was run over in a scrimmage play and knocked out. Willie Walls, a former teammate of Manton's at T.C.U., ran over to pick up his buddy. Manton came to with his eyelids flickering. Walls laughed and commented: "His eyes are ticking like a clock. Look at those glassy eyes. They look like agates."

Someone else shouted "agate-eyes" and everybody laughed, and that was Manton's nickname thereafter. Manton may have been hurt, and it was an odd thing to suggest humor. But the laugh often relieves tension on the field.

We have one incident on the field preserved in film which never fails to draw a laugh, as it did when it happened. Hube Barker tackled a fellow on a muddy field and both skidded out of bounds near our bench. Barker plowed head-on into the mud, so that he could hardly breathe. His "mud-pack" expression as he raised his face toward our bench was one of the funniest I have seen, and brought forth a spontaneous roar.

Sometimes a player can turn the laugh on the coach. Against the Eagles in Philadelphia, Kink Richards, one of our finest running backs, broke into the clear about fifty yards out and seemed sure to score a touchdown. But he set the ball down on the five-yard line, while I gasped. He was a rookie, and apparently forgot that the goal posts in professional football are on the goal line and not ten yards back, as in college. He did hold onto the ball, but he was tackled there, and I got him out of the game.

I screamed at him, and he began explaining with the words, "I thought—" He got no further because I snapped: "Never mind thinking the next time, it slows down the offense."

The next time Richards had a little trouble on the field, he was ready for me. As he trotted into the bench he yelled: "Coach, don't say a word. I was thinking again out there!" The players on the bench roared.

Such relaxation helps to take minds off the tension, and a coach will try to lighten that as much as he can. I believe in relieving the monotony of daily drill in camp too, and employ several devices to do so. For instance, every day, while we are grinding through fundamentals and putting plays together, there is a rest period, and one boy is called on to tell a story of high-school or college days which he believes to be amusing or interesting. We hear some pretty good stories, the relaxation is there, even though the whole thing may take only two minutes, and everybody gets on with the work in a relieved mood.

Rookies in particular struggle with a tremendous load in camp. For that reason we stage a special rookie show the last week in camp, at which all new men are bound to offer some sort of entertainment. Thinking for weeks about their act helps get their minds off that awful business of football. The amateur show eases tension as we move into the season. One of our smash hits of all time came in 1951, when Kyle Rote put on an imitation of me, complete with tobacco chaw in his mouth, that had the squad laughing all season.

Two years ago we trained for a while at Hershey, Pennsylvania, and the players at meals jotted down the items they ordered and signed the list, as an aid to the commissary man in figuring his output. Allie Sherman, my backfield coach, had an idea those slips would show us what kind of eaters we had on the squad, and he looked them over. To the surprise of everyone, Jimmy Ostendarp, our smallest man, was the biggest eater.

That suggested a chance to throw a light touch into a future practice, so I ordered a tremendous chocolate bar made up and presented it to Ostendarp, before the squad, at Fordham University field, where we worked on our return home. I cited him for the great battle he had put on at Hershey and expressed the hope he would continue the fight. He got the joke and so did the squad, and the following fall they were curious themselves to discover the winner of the knife-and-fork sweepstakes. My own meal check, in case my friends get any ideas, was included in the gastronomic survey.

Ostendarp's capacity at the table set me to thinking about big eaters I have known in football, certain Ivy League coaches not excepted, and I reached the surprising conclusion that the biggest man on a team seldom is its best trencherman. Generally it is a modest, medium-sized chap, whom you never would consider.

I have been trying to show that a coach is not primarily a fellow who sits up all night thinking of a master play which will win, but a very human person who has to treat with thirty to thirty-five other human beings and try to understand their personalities, so that all may work together.

A little psychology, or horse sense as we used to call it

back in the Cherokee Strip, sometimes helps when you want another fellow to go your way. Charley Avedisian, a brilliant boy as well as a good, fast guard, was quite lax in blocking on pass protection in scrimmage one day. I put up with it for a while, with the passer getting tumbled over, and then thought up a scheme to cure Charley.

I put him back to pass, and let him throw without much blocking, with my best defensive men rushing him. After fifteen minutes, he was getting groggy, and came over to me: "Coach, I see what you mean now. I'm ready to go back to guard."

We had Ed Danowski and Nello Falaschi calling signals, depending on which was in the game, when Tuffy Leemans was our best running back. Leemans, who had an astute football mind, often second-guessed the quarterback, and would try to argue him out of his call. In one game we took two penalties for too much time in the huddle because of delay, when Leemans tried to overrule Falaschi. I pulled the two over to the side lines, and said: "Leemans, from now on you are the signal-caller." He screamed over that, and said he had enough to do without calling signals. I snapped: "That's what I thought. But if you won't let anyone else call 'em, I thought you might as well do it. From now on keep your trap shut."

I winked at Danowski as I bawled Leemans out, and Ed told me later that he always had a stopper for Tuffy thereafter. When Leemans began to speak up in the huddle Ed would say: "Okay, Tuffy, you call 'em and I'll listen."

Sometimes a coach takes on a player of great talent, but cannot bring it out unless he comes close to insulting him. One of these was Jim Poole, of the Mississippi football clan, as fine an end as our team ever had. But Jim had little confidence when he reported. He was uncertain, and he could have been devastating. He missed plays because he did not realize what he could accomplish by concentrating and playing to his full capabilities.

About the third week of his first training camp, Poole still was in the fog, but I thought I had the means of bringing him through. After he failed on several plays, I lit into him. I gave it to him unmercifully before the squad, and ended with the ultimate insult of all to a good competitor: "Poole, you're not even trying."

Even before I finished Poole was stomping and snorting like a bull with a red flag before his nose. On the next play Leemans ran behind two blockers, straight for Poole. Jim drilled into that formation, and you might say he obliterated it, interference and Leemans alike.

I went over and commented sternly: "That's a little better, Jim. The next time you get in and really battle."

An alarmed Leemans piped up: "For gosh sakes, Steve, be quiet. Are you trying to get us all killed?"

That fixed up Poole's confidence. From then on the fellows playing against him were the ones who seemed to lose it when they went his way.

I mentioned Johnny Dell Isola before, as an example of the natural, instinctive, talented, and spirited football player a coach once in a great while is lucky enough to capture. Dell Isola was a rare chap who took over a position which he had never played before and held it as a regular from the first minute. Blocked off from his regular position at center by Mel Hein, he insisted in his second season, 1935, that he definitely would retire if I could not find a place for him in the lineup. I thought I had a way to cool him off.

I started Dell Isola at guard in the first game and left him in the whole sixty minutes. That was punishment, and he could hardly drag himself into the clubhouse. I complimented him on a fine game and asked: "Which is easier, playing guard or sitting it out?" He answered wryly: "Steve, I'm ready to sit for a long time."

He wasn't, of course. He was the regular guard from then on.

In that same year Dell Isola brought up an incident which caused me to formulate broad rules of conduct for the players which I have not changed through the years.

We won a particularly fine victory one Sunday, and that night as I was strolling back to the hotel after dinner, I spotted a fellow, who looked remarkably like Dell Isola, carrying a small keg of beer. He ducked into a doorway, and I was sure then that it was Johnny.

I had a good idea what was going on, but I just went into the lobby and took a seat and awaited developments. A bellhop left the hotel suddenly and returned with the keg. About five minutes later Dell Isola strolled in extra-casually and whistling. He gave me a cheery greeting and went upstairs, to follow the keg, I didn't doubt.

For about ten minutes I thought things over. Remember, I was the new coach. Playing, rather than coaching, had been in my bones until the 1933 season. I reasoned that, as a coach, I certainly wanted to know what was going on with my squad. I didn't want to be left out of anything. Also, as a coach, it seemed about time I got to some definite rules of conduct for this team. If they began slipping kegs of beer into the hotel, thinking they were fooling the coach, it wouldn't be long until they put one another up to something more than beer-running.

Then I went upstairs and found the party simply by locating the noisiest room. I walked in. Dell Isola and a group of six or seven other fellows tried to hide their glasses. However, Jim Lee Howell, end, and now our end coach, had his back to me. He was demanding another beaker of suds with all the confidence of a member of the Arkansas legislature, which he actually became.

When Howell turned around and spotted me, his expression was so funny that I had to laugh. Big Jim, six feet five, looked like a kid caught in the jam closet.

I sat down and asked for a glass of beer. I talked for a while about the fine win we had scored that day, and how I felt like celebrating too after something as grand as that. I was softening them up to get my point over.

But I said that any player who thought he was putting anything over on the coach was going to get in awful bad with me. I didn't object to a mild celebration a week before the next game, but I didn't want to have any outsider coming in and surprising me by tattling about a party my boys were holding without my knowledge.

I had their attention, and I laced it into them then. I said that I was not going to lay down any hard and fast rules for them. They were old enough to know what they wanted, and if they were going to get out of condition, I would find that out fast on the field, and I would assume they didn't want to play football.

There was only one rule they had to observe. They had to conduct themselves as gentlemen at all times. There wouldn't be a single excuse taken for violation of that rule. Any violation made the whole team and the coach and Mr. Mara look bad. It simply could not and would not happen if a boy wanted to remain on the club.

I explained to them that they were big heroes with a lot of good kids wherever they went, and that any misconduct would hurt those kids. Another thing, kids imitate their heroes, and I didn't want any kid to do anything which wasn't nice because he had seen a Giant doing it. I told them I didn't care how they treated themselves—I would find that out—but if they did anything in public to hurt impressionable kids who idolized them, the coach would ask for an accounting.

I believe the Giants, as a team, have acted like gentlemen ever since. I have an idea it was a hardship for a few, but the percentage of natural gentlemen is very high, and very satisfactory.

I believe that 1934 season was the one in which I began to act the part of a coach. Mr. Mara had said he was tired of buying uniforms for me, but I had insisted on playing through 1932 and 1933. I discovered that wouldn't work. I was amazed at what a lot of duties the coach could find just sitting on the bench.

However, the old gladiator in me did not retire gracefully, and I mixed it up with the boys in scrimmage for several years after. I thought I was in very good condition, and still quite rugged, although I may not have looked it because I was putting on some weight.

I had to be taught to give up physical contact, and it remained for Ward Cuff to give me my lesson. We worked in camp without pads, and I played opposite Cuff. In blocking me out of one play, Ward hit me in the thigh and I got a Charley horse. I didn't let on, but stopped running plays right there. I told the squad to run around the field. As they did, I tried to recover. After the squad had gone in I limped to the dressing room. I waited until the players were through with the trainer, Charley Porter, and then swore him to secrecy before letting him work over my thigh. I never did tell Cuff about that until much later. I guess I didn't fool him much, because he said he thought it was strange the way I suddenly had withdrawn from scrimmaging.

I reached the conclusion right after Cuff hit me that my

active football was ended. I had tackled Bronko Nagurski time and again and lived to tell the tale. So Cuff hadn't hurt me so much, I concluded. My own physique had simply let me down. The legs were losing their snap, and it was time to hang up my shoes for once and for all.

When I sat down as a bench coach in '34, I began to study football for the first time. I realized that no matter how much I thought I had known up to that time, most of it was concerned with mechanics of play on the field. As a coach I began to develop the over-all conception of the game, and to see it from the different points of view of eleven players on offense and eleven on defense.

Football is such a varied and interesting game that a fellow can never run out of new slants on it. I tried to get them all, and never missed a chance to see a game, whether sandlot, high-school, college, or pro. I figured they all could show me something I didn't know. They still can.

6

———————

WHEN I WAS A PLAYER I OFTEN OVERHEARD FANS DISCUSSING a game in which I had taken a hand. They didn't talk it up my way, and I often said smugly to myself: "What game were they watching?"

With the broader view of a coach, I found that fans now and then would spot an incident in a game which I had not observed, and which could be informative and helpful.

As a coach I began to realize that nobody is smart enough to see the whole of a football game. There are too many angles to consider, and a man can't be in a half-dozen locations at the same time.

The quarterback in action has one view, and his coach on the side lines another. The upstairs phone man, who completes the team of observers directing the game, has his own point of view. Then there is the scout, who has a specialized job to do for the future. In the stands we have the fans, who see it their way, and the visiting coaches and experts, who have another slant.

Sometimes I think football is a difference-of-opinion sport in which each eyewitness sees exactly what he is looking for. He sees it his way and sometimes the way he *wants* to see it. My favorite story on that point concerns our 9–7 win over the Redskins in the Polo Grounds in 1939, which brought us the eastern title.

In the closing minutes Bo Russell, of Washington, tried a field goal which would have beat us, if good. Bill Halloran, referee, called it no goal. That started quite a fuss. The Redskins were so sure Russell had made it that Ed Justice took out after Halloran when the game ended. The papers throughout the country printed a picture of the attempt, which proved the kick had hit or missed, depending on how you wanted to look at it. Russell's try was one of the most provocative episodes in league history. George Marshall, the Redskins' president, insists to this day Halloran was wrong and will exhibit pictures in support, with or without provocation.

Several years later Frank Filchock came to the Giants from the Redskins. He had been on the opposing side when Russell made his memorable kick. One day in training our gang began talking about the attempt and put a little pressure on Filchock for his opinion. Frank thought it over, and came up with as diplomatic an answer as ever I heard.

"You know, fellows," he replied, "when I was down in Washington, I felt sure that kick was good. But now that I'm up here, it's a funny thing, but I'm beginning to change my mind. I think Russell missed that kick."

Getting back to the game, there are so many things going on in sixty minutes that the full story seldom is pieced together until several accounts from various angles are considered. Movies, of course, are invaluable to hindsight wisdom, but I am considering here the eyewitness approach.

The quarterback on the field has the best view of the game to take advantage of a momentary lapse by the opposition. He can change a play while calling signals to capitalize on a wrong move being made at that instant. Nobody else can; all others trail the action. That is why I like my quarterback to call the plays, as far as he can go, rather than depend on messengers shuttling in and out with bench directions. That is, of course, assuming I have a boy out there with sound judgment.

The phone man, looking down on the field and in constant touch with the bench, watches the position of players on both sides, in relation to each other. He is on the alert for overshifted defenses. A defense man may be several yards too shallow, deep, close, or wide to stop a particular play which we know is in the offensive team's repertory and which we expect to be used. The halfbacks are most often guilty of that fault. Speaking of Filchock reminds me of the game in '46 in which he was hailed as a hero for his excellent running against his former Redskin teammates.

Filchock owed an assist to our phone man that day. The upstairs observer had spotted their left tackle playing three or four yards wide. Taking quick advantage of the information, Filchock barreled through the hole for several long gains. Our phone man was more observing than their phone man.

The coach is not in the most favorable spot to get a picture of the game. He often has awkward angles of view, and he is on a level with the action, so that players often cut him off from a play on the opposite side of the field.

In one close game in the Polo Grounds, Tuffy Leemans caught a punt and started down our side of the field. From where I stood, I thought he had a good opening in the direction he took.

I yelled: "This way, this way, Tuffy!"

He cut back to the other side line instead and went

sixty for a touchdown. When he came back to the bench he looked at me slyly and said: "Coach, I heard you, but from where I was I could see a lot more daylight on the other side."

Tuffy was right, of course. He could see the whole field; I saw only part of it.

Thereafter, I reserved my advice until we looked at the movies. Then, when a fellow missed an opening, I could second-guess him without a comeback.

Another time, in Pittsburgh, Ward Cuff tried a forty-yard field goal from an angle on the opposite side of the field. I thought the ball went under the crossbar, and was sure of that when I failed to see an official signal that it was good. My boys came running back to line up for a kickoff and I shouted: "Where do you think you are going—that ball is being put in play on the twenty!"

Cuff shouted back: "Why, Coach, I made that one."

"Not from where I'm standing," I retorted.

He pointed to the scoreboard. The three-pointer was up there. I guess I was the only person in the park who didn't think the kick was good.

Coaches on their day off in the stands, and others closely identified with the game, generally prefer to sit in the end zone. I never fail to spot a group of college coaches around Section 22 in the Polo Grounds, which is the "old pro" area behind the end line. From that head-on view they can see the spacing of the lines, the development of the blocking for break-throughs, and other tactics especially interesting to them.

The fan, on the other hand, wants to sit on the fifty-yard line and likes to keep his eyes on the ball. He can probably relate more about those who handle the ball—runners, passers, receivers—than any other type of observer. Sports writers usually sit there too, because their stories are mostly about the progress of the ball and the player directly responsible for the progress.

The scout hardly ever concentrates on the ball-handler. He is more interested in what makes the ball go. He wants the cold dope, the mass of detail, which will permit him to analyze a team's attack and defense for the future. Therefore, he looks ahead of the ball, to see the play forming. He must learn the pattern or design of play, particularly on passes, because this is fundamental knowledge, usually useful for the entire season.

Those are the various ways a person may look at a football game. I believe the average fan is eager to see as much as he can, and more than he does, on the gridiron, because an abiding question in my mail through the years can be boiled down to this: "How should I watch a football game?"

Another perennial favorite with the public is the role of the scout, who is regarded as a mysterious fellow, and the value of his job toward winning a game.

Let's take up the spectator approach to the game first. The fan, when he focuses all attention on the ball, misses the mechanics which make plays work.

Carrying the ball isn't a difficult job—it isn't very heavy. Anybody ought to be able to move it along. But up ahead is where the men do the work to clear a path for the ball and the chap who carries it. They are the men who make possible 90 to 95 per cent of a team's successful plays. Only the extraordinary player, of superior ability, can gain much more than his teammates can earn for him.

Fans can have more fun at football, and understand better how the game works, if they will look ahead of the ball-carrier. As Jack Lavelle, our chief scout, puts it: "Watch the line and you won't miss the ball—it's bound to get there one way or another."

It's true the coach has an advantage over the spectator in looking ahead, because he has a pretty good idea what play the quarterback will call in a certain situation and he knows the assignments on that play. For instance, through long practice, I can tell most of the time what all eleven Giants have done in any particular play.

Even though they don't have this inside knowledge, spectators will discover football is a game of patterns, and that it is easy to get the hang of them, both in the blocking formations and in the deployment of receivers for a pass. The average fan will have a good idea of a team's technique after he sees the "works" go round for five or six home games. He will be talking like an expert, about what could have happened as well as what did happen.

Some of the regular Giant fans have learned to look ahead; but many still concentrate on the ball. I know that because I receive letters from year to year demanding more "deception" in our attack. That is the curse of a coach with his home fans, the insistence on more "deception." No matter what system he uses, the fans see it so often they become accustomed to it, and look for something new.

The Giants switched from the T to my A formation in 1950 and scored more than fifty points against the Cardinals. At dinner that night a friend complimented me on the one-sided decision, but added: "Still and all, Steve, I've seen the A before, and I like something with more deception."

That stopped me for a moment, and then I said: "Look, we scored fifty points. Don't you think somebody was fooled?"

I also asked him if he believed the Cardinals' T, which didn't score very much, seemed more deceptive to him than the A. The double-barreled comeback persuaded him to concede he might have been a little hasty in junking my A formation.

That gave me a chance to explain a point which all coaches would like to get across to the fans. None of us is trying to fool the spectator in the stands; we are trying to build plays which will make eleven defensive men hesitate in doubt for one fraction of a second. That's all deception is—one brief moment of doubt. You know, he who hesitates, etc.

The backs are trying to hide the ball from eleven men, not fifty thousand. Also, spectators see the play from all angles and can afford to stay with the ball. The defensive men don't have that privilege. They have to watch blockers and fakers, more than anything else. If you can fake a 250-pound tackle out of position, that's much easier than trying to block him out. A good fake is as essential as a good block. That's deception, but it may not be observed at all by many of the thousands in the stands.

I illustrated deception one night on Giant Quarterback Huddle, my television show, and was amazed to find the stunt more popular than anything we had demonstrated all season.

I put on a center and four backs—without the benefit of a line to hide them—BUT I had them face the cameras, so that the viewers would be in the position of the defensive team, and not in the side-line seats where deception loses value.

The boys ran through the same play three times, with a different back taking the ball each time from the quarterback. The play would be stopped for a few seconds before revealing the ball, to give viewers a chance to guess.

My mail indicated the show was a hit, but I knew it would be before it went on. As we ran through plays in rehearsal, for the director to check his camera angles, we gradually picked up an audience from the studio force. Many were frank to say they never thought of football and deception in that way, from the point of view of the men who had to stop it.

I think any fan will find it a treat to look ahead of the ball the next time. If he sees defense men going in the wrong direction, and big holes opening in the line, and linemen desperately striving to catch up with a play which has struck in their area, then he can be sure an attack packs a lot of deception for the men it is intended to fool. He will look in vain, however, for any attack which can mystify all the fans in the stands.

I would like to put in a few extra words about fans, if they don't mind.

In the old days there were many unruly customers. I remember a game in Rock Island, Illinois, at which the police cleared the field three times. After the game ended we kept our helmets on in the bus because unhappy home fans, who had probably lost two bucks, were throwing rocks through the windows. We hunched up in our seats to avoid a brick in the back of the neck. "Rock" Island indeed!

I think fans are just as enthusiastic today. But maybe there are more cops, because rocks are no longer a menace.

However, a few fans abuse players through their unkind language, and I always did think that was unfair. The only time I concede fans have a right to get on a boy is when he is not doing his best. But in that case I'll guarantee the coach will begin to scorch his hide before the fans get around to it.

Generally, a player is hustling and trying and wants to win, and when he makes a mistake it isn't on purpose. Then, too, fans may not know the whole story when a man doesn't seem up to his best. He may be playing with an injury or may have trouble in the family, but feels it his duty to go out and play, even though his whole mind cannot be on the field.

I have known many professional athletes since I joined the Cowboys in 1924, and I am convinced all but a very, very small number had enough pride in looking good to do their best at all times.

In football you will often see a man play below form because he refuses to quit with an injury. Nello Falaschi, among the most reliable and hardest-hitting blocking backs in league history, loved so well to play that he once hid a very badly injured leg from me, and started a game. He was obviously in agony, but when I took him out after five minutes or so he was heartbroken.

Chuck Conerly did not do his usual excellent passing job in '51, particularly on the long throws. But there was a story to that which was a tribute to Conerly.

He suffered a shoulder separation in a preseason game. We expected to lose him for two to three weeks of the regular season, but he was on me right at the start to go in the opener. The doctor wasn't too eager for it, but I did let Conerly work about five minutes, and he went on from there. He had a very painful shoulder for the better part of the season, but never complained.

I knew right off that he wasn't as loose as he claimed. I saw him clutch that shoulder several times after throwing and bend over in pain, in the first few games. I didn't mention that to him. I also found out that Chuck was going to a doctor regularly for treatment, long after he assured me he had no more trouble, but I didn't let on about that either. After the season, when he could not be in the position of offering an alibi, he confessed the shoulder had not been right until the very close of the schedule.

Then I told him I had known it all the while and had respect for the way he carried through. Conerly took criticism and some abuse from the stands, when he obviously failed to make the long hard throw to ends who were open. He took it in silence. I knew, and he knew, that we would have lost several games that we won, if he had begged off. Had Chuck not been injured we might have won the championship, because time and again our ends were open for shots which he would have completed with ease the year before.

Tom Landry, one of our defense stars at halfback, was another who insisted on playing in 1951, although he might have been pardoned for laying off several games because of a succession of injuries to one knee. He was unable to punt with that knee, but wasn't willing to sit out. He intercepted two passes for touchdowns, even though he could not run at full speed.

I could go on for a long while telling of men who insisted on doing their best for the team although injured, and who took abuse at times from the stands rather than crawl into a corner with an alibi.

Now and then a player simply cannot take it any longer. In 1951, for instance, Val Jansante, an end who had given full value for years to the Pittsburgh Steelers, quit rather than undergo mounting criticism from the fans. Art Rooney, Pittsburgh president, understood Jansante's predicament and arranged for him to go over to Green Bay, so that he could continue playing—and make a living.

I believe Polo Grounds fans are as tolerant a group as you will find anywhere, but still and all they had an effect on Em Tunnell, our brilliant broken-field runner on punt returns, which caused me no end of worry. It actually contributed to at least one defeat with a direct bearing on the title.

In Em's first season, 1948, he made a fair catch of a punt. He was soundly booed. The fans did not realize Tunnell was under orders to fair-catch. All my players are instructed to take no chances with punts, because the average runback is very small, and the risk of a fumble for the sake of gaining a few additional yards is too large. In fact, our two receivers work as a team. The one who stands by to block or take a handoff is to yell at the receiver whether to fair-catch or run, and he is to call the safety-first play if in doubt.

But Em couldn't abide that booing. He insisted he didn't want anybody to think he was a sissy. I respected that attitude; I wanted him to feel manly about it. I didn't order him to fair-catch, but tried week after week to convince him that it was the smart and profitable way to handle punts in the long run, unless there was a definite opening for a gain.

Three years later, the memory of that booing was still with him, and he would not give the fair-catch signal unless he was about to be smothered. Because of that, he fumbled a punt on which he had no chance to run in our game in Cleveland in 1951. The Browns recovered and were off to an easy touchdown in a game we lost by 14–13!

The reaction of the fans at a game can have a definite effect on some players. It has very little effect on me because I have a job to do, and if I listen to the advice from the stands I may not be able to do it.

As a coach, I regard scouting as an essential in planning for any game. The football sleuth's job now is a highly specialized one. His report is quite a bit more comprehensive than the first advance information I heard about an upcoming foe.

That was back at Phillips U., in my first season under Johnny Maulbetsch. We were surprised one day to see our president, Dr. I. N. McCash, come on the practice field. He knew little of athletics, although he was strongly in favor of organized competition, and he left the coaching to Maulbetsch as a rule.

The squad gathered to hear the prexy's message. He told Maulbetsch he had been traveling and had seen a team we were to play, and thought he ought to pass on whatever information he had. His report went: "Well, Coach, they take that ball and try to run with it most of the time, they throw it sometimes, and once in a while they kick."

I am not poking fun at Dr. McCash. He is a very enthusiastic supporter of sports, and one of the finest gentlemen I have known. But his idea of football was just about all the average fellow knew about it in our country in the old rough-and-tumble times.

I tell the story because I sometimes feel, when I have depended on a detailed and comprehensive scouting report too heavily, that I would have been better off with one on the McCash style.

That's because scouting can be overdone when we know so much about a team that we begin to work up defenses for special plays they have. They may never run one of their specials, and you wind up worrying about nothing. If we follow the report only so far as the fundamental plays, with variations, we have put our time to best effect.

We had a very thorough report on Detroit for a game in the Polo Grounds some years ago. Gus Dorais coached the Lions, and he had developed a terrific pass attack, with lots of speed, and with Frankie Sinkwich throwing. From the single wing he could sneak out delayed receivers, so that he had five downfield on almost every pass. Our offensive squad simulated the Dorais attack, and in two days of practice our defense platoon was never able to cover. A receiver was always open.

If this continued, someone would go mad, and I didn't want it to be me. I called the team together and instructed: "We cannot cover all those fellows, so let's not cover any of them. Forget the scouting report and act as if we never heard about the Lions. We will rush the passer, play the ball, forget about man-to-man coverage, and use a zone defense."

We shut them out.

But I wouldn't want to open up blind, without benefit of scouting, as a custom.

Jock Sutherland scoffed at scouting reports—just once—and regretted it. That was when the doctor first joined the pros to coach Brooklyn. He had never seen Don Hutson, all-time great receiver, who starred for the Packers. He refused to believe it was necessary to assign two men to guard him. Everybody else in the league used two, and sometimes three, against Hutson, and he still could beat them. But Sutherland insisted he never saw anybody he ever had to cover with two men, and that his defenders were good enough to handle Hutson.

And so Brooklyn played Green Bay in Milwaukee with one Sutherland defender on Hutson. Don caught the first three passes Cecil Isbell threw, and ran for three touchdowns. He made the doc change his mind right away.

Sutherland often brought up that game when we had a session in later years, and he repeated time and again that he never had seen anything in his life like Hutson that day.

Scouting today is highly specialized, and a scout has to have peculiar talent. Some of our best football players and sound coaches cannot do a competent job. They cannot get that complete summary of the play which the top sleuth delivers to his coach. That takes practice and work, and plenty of both. Movies aid immensely in preparing for a game, but the personal appraisal of an opponent is still vital.

The good scouting report presents as complete a picture as man can provide. I have just run down one of Jack Lavelle's layouts. Let me mention some of the topics. Condition of field . . . Weather . . . Wind direction and force . . . Sequence in which plays were run . . . Description of plays . . . Defense against those plays . . . Pass patterns . . . Favorite receivers . . . Analysis of runners, as to their pet plays, and whether any will run better to one side than to the other . . . The bread-and-butter play for first downs with a yard or two to go . . . Diagrams of basic plays and variations to watch . . . Percentage of passes thrown to number of running plays . . . Complete report on personnel, by position and number . . . Estimate of speed of opponents, compared man for man with Giants . . . Their defense formations against all types of plays . . . Their reaction, individually, to passes . . . And so on. It is marvelous that a top scout can train himself to observe so much.

The ultimate knowledge which a coach obtains from a good scouting job is the breakdown into patterns of an opponent's offense and defense. That is why I insist football is a simple game, despite all the technical language associated with it. Players have to go to their strength, where they will gain the most, and you can bet they will do so virtually every time they have the ball. And teams must call their best play, the one with the most chance to gain, when they are in tight spots. That's just like a base-ball pitcher using his best pitch in the clutch. He simply cannot afford to fool around or be fancy.

Therefore, with a good scouting report before him, the

coach will build his defense to stop the opponent's strength. He will be more than willing to take a chance on surprises. If he can make the other fellow go away from his obvious strength, then he is away ahead.

The two games the Giants won from the Cleveland Browns in 1950, by 6–0 and 17–13, caused general surprise. We weren't supposed to do that. Only a very few teams had ever beaten the Browns. No one ever did it twice in a season. No club ever had shut them out. Scouting had a lot to do with our success.

To begin with, I had several good defense men who had worked against the Browns in Otto Schnellbacher, Tom Landry, Harmon Rowe, and Arnie Weinmeister. Naturally, they contributed what they knew to start the pot boiling. They were valuable on details, in briefing our squad on traits and tricks of the Browns which they had observed on the field.

We did not have movies of the Browns to study, nor did they have films of us, because we had never met and league rules permit movies only of games in which a team has played.

On scouting, we saw the Browns as often as we could. Lavelle caught them five times. I saw them three times. Our coaching staff saw them twice. When we all sat down together two weeks before our first game, we were able to pool our information and arrive at definite conclusions and a formal defense.

Our main conclusion was this: to beat Cleveland we had to stop their chief offensive weapon which was their passing. We had to devise a defense in which we could have more men deep, without weakening our defense against running. They were able to run with six boys, including powerful Marion Motley and speedy Dub Jones. We would have to try to double-team, in certain situations, their dangerous receivers, Dante Lavelli, Mac Speedie, both ends, and Jones, a halfback. We would have to throw against them, if possible, something they had not played before.

We finally arrived at a 6-1-4 defense, which means six men on the line, one backer-up, and four men deep to guard against passes. But this was to be a flexible formation, which could be switched on command to 4-1-6, 5-1-5, or 5-2-4, depending on their success at the start.

We intended to stay in the 6-1-4 until they made us get out of it. They didn't in that first game, and we therefore reserved our variations for the second game.

In the first game we covered their receivers at all times but did not put much pressure on Otto Graham, their quarterback and passer in the T formation. Our ends, Jim Duncan and Ray Poole, who had followed his brother Jim to the Giants, would slide and float and drop off with receivers. Although they did this, to give us a virtual four-man line, with Al DeRogatis and Weinmeister, tackles, and Jon Baker and John Mastrangelo, guards, we were able to hold their running often enough to control it. John Cannady, backer-up, was assigned to cover Motley, and stay with him on running plays or on the screen pass, which he could make so deadly.

In the first half, Graham tried to throw long, and did not complete a pass, and their runners tried to work through our four-man line.

Now, all quarterbacks and coaches go in a huddle at the half, to figure out how to beat the defense, from what they have learned. Sometimes there is not enough time to work out a complete plan. But you can bet that when you play the same team again they will have something cooked up to outwit your defense, if you don't change also.

In the second half of the 6–0 game, Brown altered his

attack to throw short passes and run wide. The 6-1-4 held, because Poole and Duncan, instead of peeling off with receivers, drove in on ball-carriers trying to get outside them, and Landry and Rowe, our defensive halfbacks, came up for the tackle once the threat of passing ended. Tunnell and Schnellbacher, the deep men in the so-called "umbrella" quartet in the backfield, still had the deep pass threat under control.

When we came up to the second game, naturally I expected something surprising from a coach as shrewd as Paul Brown. But the Browns had shown us nothing which voided our original scouting data, and I wanted to find a way to keep that 6-1-4 as my basic formation.

I had to figure that, if we played it the same way as we did in the 6–0 game, Brown would take advantage of our ends dropping off to throw short passes and to double-team our exposed tackles so that they could not rush Graham. I also had to figure that if Cannady shadowed Motley, as he had in the first game, Brown would be sure to throw counter plays at the position our backer-up vacated, by using Motley as a decoy.

What we decided was to stay in 6-1-4, but with our ends crashing in on Graham rather than floating. Cannady would cover Motley closely, though only in certain situations, so that they could not count on it. But even with these radical changes in tactics, we didn't want to let Brown see 6-1-4 all through the game. We didn't want him to know we were committed to the one formation. As variations, we decided to pull one guard out of the line to backer-up for a 5-2-4 when running seemed their best suit, and to take out a guard and put in an extra halfback for a 5-1-5 when passing seemed their most profitable lead.

We were able to pay off on these changes, because they

had not counted on our ends crashing. Their blocking was set up for drifting ends and, as I suspected, to work on our tackles. They had great difficulty readjusting to block on our ends, who drove in hard, and who were able to throw Graham for a total loss of seventy-eight yards.

On attack, the Browns did throw short, and did try the delayed counter plays, but our defense had enough variety so that they could not figure Cannady's role. It was not the fault of our defense that they led 13–3 at the half, because an error by one of our men (Ostendarp) gave them the ball, and a touchdown from our one-yard line just as the first half ended.

When we scored to make it 13–10 in the third period, our defense again paid off. Brown no longer had a safe lead, because he did not want a tie, as we had beat them in the first game on their field. So he began to throw long, and our secondary picked off three passes, which enabled us to maintain ball possession for a wide majority of the time.

Scouting was the basis of those two wins, because we had judged the strong points of the Browns accurately and were able to contain them.

Now I will cite an instance which our scouting did not cover, in the 8–3 defeat we suffered in Cleveland in the play-off for the American Conference championship. It turned out to be a fatal flaw.

On a frozen field, the teams were tied at 3–3 in the fourth period. We had lost a touchdown, Conerly to Bob McChesney, on a careless offside which had no part in the play, and that was the only chance we were to have.

But Graham made the difference for the Browns. Apparently bogged down in their own territory, Otto rushed the ball in field-goal range for Lou Groza, and they took a 6–3 lead. The safety scored against us later was meaningless, because it came from desperation in the final seconds.

Graham won on brilliant delayed runs down the middle. We had never seen him in that role, nor did our scouting make note of it. Of course we knew about his quarterback sneak; that is a standard play. But ingenious Otto on that bleak December day made his fakes, held for a count, and then wheeled to go through the middle, as our guards, committed on the icy ground, rushed past him. If we had known about this play, we probably could have kept him from field-goal range. But the play was superbly executed, as a surprise, with perfect timing, and was a tribute to Brown's coaching and to Graham's quality as a player. It was the play which made them champions that day.

Scouting in the early days was rudimentary, and movies were not used in football. Teams often played each other sight unseen. They tell a story about Lone Star Dietz which illustrates that point. Lone Star was an Indian who played at Carlisle under Pop Warner and who coached Haskell. Like Warner, and also Bob Zuppke, he was an artist in oils and water color as well as one in football. Dietz was George Marshall's coach when the Redskins represented Boston, and I believe Marshall still regards him as his best. When the Redskins played the Bears in Boston, Dietz knew little about the Halas system.

He graciously offered Halas the use of the park the day before the game. While they drilled, Dietz was stretched out on the roof observing. After the Bears left, Lone Star called his boys in, revised defenses, and scored a notable upset the following day. That's what I am told. There would be no need to go to that extreme in these times. Scouting is so thorough that you can know without seeing what a team is going to do the day before a game. They are going to run through their plays, to loosen up, and a scout wouldn't see anything he didn't already know.

When the Giants played the Redskins in Boston, Dietz got the surprise of his life. He wanted to work the upstairs phone and coach from there, and when he left he instructed his team to kick off. By the time he got to the phone on the roof, the Redskins were receiving.

He assailed his assistant coach: "What's going on down there? Didn't I tell you to kick off?"

The assistant glumly replied: "We did, Coach. The score is 7–0."

Harry Newman of the Giants had run back the kickoff for a touchdown.

Curly Lambeau, of Green Bay, was another coach who for a while preferred to coach from the upstairs phone. The advantage is that you can see, from that height, how both teams are deployed. You are in position to order a play with more personal knowledge than is possible on the bench. But I believe the disadvantage of being out of close contact with the team far outweighs any benefit. Also, if you do not have a good assistant coach to do a job on the phone you are worse off letting him go downstairs where he has the direct supervision of the team.

Lambeau coached from the press box at the Polo Grounds in 1949, and, when he left just before the half to come down to the dressing room, he took a ramp which led him out of the park. He rushed to the visiting clubhouse and banged on the outside door, but nobody pays any attention to knocks there. It could be an army of indignant fans bent on destruction of the coach. Poor Curly didn't have a ticket or identification on him. He hurried to the press gate and tried to explain who he was.

Ernie Viberg, long a familiar figure at the Polo Grounds, had charge of the gate. An unexcitable Scandinavian, his specialty is turning down numerous characters who claim in one way or another that their presence is essential. He had seen a long procession of "experts" file through to sit in judgment on this particular game.

One more "coach" at half time was one too many for Ernie.

He listened to Lambeau's tearful plea and turned him down: "So you're the coach? Mister, I have met a number of football coaches today. And not a one got through this gate!"

Someone finally recognized Curly, and he "crashed" the gate. But he got back in the park just in time to see his men leave the dressing room for the second half. After that he avoided the press box. He went down on the bench, which is the proper place for the coach, and the place he ultimately takes, no matter how many experiments he may try. Ray Flaherty, coach of the Yankees in the All-America Conference, once used a TV set on the side lines to get an upstairs view of the game. But he could not watch the picture and the field at once. The coach has only one pair of eyes and cannot see everything that goes on. He must have help from the eyes of the scout, of the quarterback, of his phone man, and occasionally of the knowing fan.

When he puts all the "views" together properly in his composite picture, he's lucky. When he doesn't, he might just as well coach, like Lambeau, from outside the park.

7

⌇⌇⌇⌇⌇⌇⌇⌇⌇⌇⌇

STYLES IN FOOTBALL CHANGE LIKE VOGUES IN LADIES' HATS.
A coach can come up with outstanding personnel who
have the training and the teamwork to win handsomely.
But they may not receive full credit, because folks will
assume it's the formation they use which makes the difference. The new fashion always catches the eye.

Pop Warner came east with Stanford to play Army in
1926. He had a great ball club and defeated a good Army
team and made them look bad. Warner used the double
wing, and there was a pell-mell rush to that formation.
Few stopped to realize the coach wouldn't have been in
double wing if he didn't have an all-time fullback, Ernie
Nevers, to make the formation work. Nevers was a perfect
fit; he made the double wing stylish.

In 1941 Clark Shaughnessy coached another great Stanford team to a somewhat surprising win over Nebraska
in the Rose Bowl, and there was another rush, this time
to the T. Again, the folks didn't appreciate that Shaughnessy had four backs—Albert, Standlee, Gallarneau,
Kmetovic—who were terrific operators in the T. They
made the formation seem the most brilliant and over-
powering ever used. The T swept the country.

The split T, in which the linemen are separated from
one another in varying degrees and not packed shoulder-

to-shoulder on each side of center, came in a few years later and grew increasingly popular. Why? Because several coaches, notably Don Faurot of Missouri, Bud Wilkinson of Oklahoma, and Jim Tatum of Maryland, achieved unusual success with it.

In the Southwest, spread formations in which there is extraordinary spacing between linemen, and backs too, became the rage because Dutch Meyer at Texas Christian and Matty Bell at Southern Methodist, among others, made it an exciting and profitable system.

In 1950 the T began to tail off somewhat, and the single wing, which had always been with us, came back to fashion, because of the same old reason for football styles—coaches had discovered players peculiarly fitted to excel in that formation. Dick Kazmaier, for instance, became a national name in single wing under Charlie Caldwell at Princeton.

In 1951 the trend was toward a combination system of T and single wing. Biggy Munn at Michigan State used both T and single wing with a buck lateral series, and did a remarkable job in keeping defenses off balance. The defense wasn't puzzled over the plays that would be run from either system; it just wasn't fast enough to adjust from one formation to the other.

Several more coaches who brought back the single wing, either straightaway or in combination with the T, were Bob Neyland of Tennessee, Jesse Hill of Southern California, and Red Sanders of U.C.L.A. Rusty Russell at S.M.U. used the T with spreads. The headlines their teams made started a new trend, and in 1952 college football was in a transition period, with coaches long committed to one system willing to try a little bit of everything.

This willingness to experiment is the healthiest thing that's happened to football in a long while. When there is a craze for one system, as there was for so long for the T, all football tends to be tied up. There is no variety. The college coach gets boys from high school who have been trained in the T, and, rather than start over with them, he goes along with the T. The coach in the pros has even less choice, because when he gets a boy after seven or eight years in the T, he just doesn't have much chance, and surely not the time, to change him over. He has to follow the fashion.

Eddie Price, fullback who led the league in rushing for the Giants in 1951, is an extraordinary case. Eddie grew up in high school and at Tulane in the T, yet had little difficulty fitting into the A formation, which is my invention off the single wing. We used both T and A in 1951, and Price gained equally well in both formations. Seldom will a coach find a boy so adaptable, even if he has the enthusiasm to learn.

But the Pittsburgh Steelers, traditionally a single-wing team, had to abandon that formation because they couldn't find enough competent boys who had been trained in their system. The T craze had virtually driven single wing out of the high schools. However, with the new freedom of formations in 1952, it seemed likely that single-wing boys would be available again in a short while.

I looked on that prospect with pleasure, because my A formation and the single wing require a cracking good blocking back, and that sort of individual had been the rarest number in the sport for a period of ten years.

The Giants used the A and the T in 1950, and I began mixing in double-wing plays in 1951. Then, when we drafted Fred Benners, of S.M.U., for the 1952 season, I had visions of playing him in the Southwest spreads to which he was accustomed. Then we would have the use of four formations in our attempts to jab the offense off stride.

However, if I had a dozen formations, I couldn't win if I didn't have players who could block and tackle. Those are the fundamentals of the game. A coach has to come up against the two, and win or lose because of the two, no matter how ingenious he may be. When boys come to me for advice I tell them that they will have a chance on any ball club if they can block and tackle, and that they won't make any club if they can't.

Here is another inescapable fact about the various systems—no matter which one a coach prefers, he has to make his off-tackle play work, or he might as well give up. It is the one which is best for those difficult yards, for first down or touchdown. It is the play which sets up all other plays, and when a club can't make it, it can't make anything else. I don't mean you have to use the off-tackle every time a first down or touchdown beckons. I do mean you have to convince the other side you can make the off-tackle, and then, with that as a valid threat, you can select other plays with a good chance of success. The off-tackle has long-gaining possibilities as well as first-down potential. It makes the defense slide to meet the runner, who has the chance to cut inside if the man he has to beat moves a step too far to the outside.

When we hear of teams claiming to have 220 or 330 attacking plays it does come rather hard to believe one play, the off-tackle, can be the key to all.

However, it isn't exactly truthful to claim 220 or 330 plays. Football is based on no more than ten essential plays, and the rest of the huge total in an attacking portfolio are variations of those fundamental plays.

There are four essential running plays, the off-tackle, the quick opener, the end run, and the counter.

Add four passing plays, for hook, fan, crossover, and screen passes.

Complete the list with two kicking formations, for punt and place kick.

After those, all others are variations.

The off-tackle, as already pointed out, is the bread-and-butter play of any system, or any good team.

The quick opener is a direct thrust through the line, in an attempt to use the straight-line, shortest distance to the goal. The term covers any number of variations. It may be a delayed quick opener, or one employed with a mouse-trap. The Giants, for instance, use "veer" plays off the quick opener. In these, the ball-carrier heads for the point he normally hits, but veers to left or right to strike in another position just before he reaches the line. That is a change-of-pace which all attacks must have to avoid being typed.

The end run is the opposite of the quick opener, because it involves running around a defense, rather than through it, and naturally demands speed. If a team doesn't have the speed to run wide, it is in grave trouble, because the defense will overshift to cover other plays and hug the attack to death. An end run has to be turned downfield as fast as possible, because if a back runs too long laterally, toward the side line, he will have the entire defense jammed in on him when he does make his turn.

The counter is the sucker play. It aims to hit at a spot vacated by a lineman or backer-up who has been lured out of position by a fake at another point. Some fans may recognize it better by the old name, cross buck. The reverse play of the single wing is a counter. All variations of the counter are designed to "hit where they ain't."

For example, one back fakes taking the ball and strikes between center and his left guard, hoping to fool the backer-up on that side. A fraction of a second later the real ball-carrier will drive through a hole made by his left tackle and left end, at the spot the backer-up held originally.

A hook, or buttonhook pass, takes its name from the path of the receiver, generally the end, which resembles an old-fashioned buttonhook. He runs straight out for five to ten yards, then turns about-face to his inside to catch the pass. It is a short-gaining pass essentially, for the first down. Yet it has a variation called hook-and-go, in which the end does not complete his about-face and tries to maintain stride for a further gain.

A fan pass is so called because it is generally thrown to any of three receivers who attempt to flood an area while fanning out to the side line. It is also known as a down-and-out pass, because the receiver usually catches it after he has flared from his downfield course, but just as he is about to go out of bounds. This is a good gainer in smart hands, because the receiver can count on having his body between the ball and the defender, and the passer has the side line working for him because an overshoot will be out of bounds. If the defending halfback charges between the receiver and the ball for an interception try, he takes the risk of letting the catcher break into the clear.

The crossover pass is designed for touchdowns. In this, the receiver cuts diagonally to his inside, with his catching point about in the center of the field, where he has maximum room to maneuver, and is also at the spot where he is most likely to shake the defense, either in man-for-man or in zone deployment. The crossover generally is combined with one or two receivers driving straight downfield on the side toward which the primary receiver is heading.

The screen pass is intended to take advantage of hard-charging opposing linemen and backers-up and to keep them "honest." After a quarterback has taken a going-over from the eagerly rushing defense for a few plays, he will have one of his backs fake a block, then slide off into the flat where he can receive the ball just after the chargers have passed him and before they hit the passer. It is combined with a lateral movement of the attacking line toward the receiver so as to provide him with downfield blocking.

Punt formation takes various forms. The short punt formation was a standard offense years ago and has been used now and then in college and pro ball in recent years. But the standard formation is intended for punting, with a tightly held blocking pocket to keep charging linemen away from the kicker.

That standard setup is giving way rapidly to the new spread punt formation, which I believe was first used successfully by Henry Frnka of Tulane about 1947. The idea here is to prevent runbacks. The opposition isn't kept out, but allowed to come in on the kicker, who is not likely to be bothered, because he punts from fourteen yards back. Meanwhile, his teammates, from their spread, are able to rush downfield to tackle the receiver. The Giants use this spread formation exclusively, and we don't block very long on anybody before the kick.

The place-kick formation is intended only for kicks for field goals and for extra points, and it must afford maximum blocking protection for the kicker seven yards behind the line.

These foundation plays developed the offshoots called variations, because defense men began to move around in the late twenties, and increasingly so in the early thirties. They refused to be sitting ducks for blocks any longer. But they switched their style only because they could no longer handle an offense which had received monumental advantages from the rules-makers.

The three radical changes in favor of offense in the

National Football League were: starting every play at least fifteen yards from the side line; permission to forward-pass anywhere behind the line of scrimmage; and the restoration of the goal posts to the goal line.

When I was a tackle, the ball had to be put in play wherever it was downed, even if that spot were only an inch removed from the side line. Obviously, that meant the offense often had to waste a down to better position by moving in toward the center line of the field. On that kind of play the fans and the defense could afford to yawn, because nothing exciting was likely to happen. Also, a team which could win or tie with a field goal toward the end of the game didn't dare try a wide play for a touchdown, for fear of being sewed into a corner, at an angle which prohibited a field goal. The offense often was cramped, under the original rule of the game.

But a team was able to run virtually any play in its catalogue when the rules decreed the ball always had to be spotted at least fifteen yards from the side line. The distance later was increased to twenty yards. Simple mathematics will show how valuable that proved on attack. The football field is 160 feet wide. With twenty-yard, or sixty-foot, alleys on each side, the ball always is snapped somewhere within a forty-foot strip down the center of the gridiron. That insures ample room on either side for end plays. It also makes field goals easier, because the angle of kicking is never acute. The only bad angle, in fact, is inside the five-yard line, and there we have the singular situation in which it is advisable to take a penalty to obtain a spot nearer a right angle to the crossbar for the placement.

When in 1933 the forward pass was permitted anywhere behind the line of scrimmage, an entirely different type of game opened up. Before that, a forward was advertised in advance, because the passer had to throw from five yards or more behind the line. He signaled his purpose when he stood back there, waiting for his receiver. With the new rule, better faking from the T was made possible, because the quarterback did not have to retreat every time he wanted to throw. Faster striking passes over the line also created a new menace to defense. In the single wing, the freedom of throwing fashioned probably the most dangerous play in football, the optional run-or-pass stratagem by the ball-receiver. In that play the left halfback or tailback may run or pass, depending on his judgment as to the best opening.

The NFL replaced the goal posts in their traditional spot on the goal line, in order to make field goals easier to score, and thus help avert tie games. Nobody loves a tie, and the NFL went far toward eliminating deadlocks. In the 1941–50 decade, for instance, there were only nineteen ties in more than 650 games, and in one season there were none.

The defense had to find some means to counteract these wonderful blessings showered on the offense. Within a limited area we had the standard old-fashioned seven-diamond or seven-box formation for a smash-and-shove type of game. This could not cope with an attack which could probe the entire field. In my time, teams were made up of foot soldiers with a few cavalrymen to ride the flanks. After 1933 air power was the theme, and the scope of the battlefield increased commensurately.

The defense had to make up in maneuvers what the rules had granted to the attack. Instead of a set seven-man line, six- and five-man lines were devised, with combinations of backers-up and secondary men. In addition, linemen began to slide and loop and drop out of the line, so as not to present stationary targets for blocking in the long-accustomed spots.

With fluid defenses, what did the offense do? Consider the off-tackle play. Instead of running time after time against a standard defense, it had to work now against five-man and six-man lines also. That meant the blocking assignments had to be changed to fit the circumstances. It also had to be altered somewhat in execution depending on the arrangement of the backers-up. Instead of one invariable play, it became one with a dozen phases. The off-tackle did not become twelve different plays, but gained flexibility so as to take account of all conditions of defense. Strategically it was the same play no matter what fancy name it took on, but tactically it had to vary to overcome the shifting defense.

These variations were worked out primarily on the field, and not in a dream world of diagrams. The players often switched blocking as they went along to try to wreck an opposing tackle who wouldn't stay put.

If a group of youngsters will practice the ten basic plays I have named, so as to run a smooth, assured attack, and is opposed by a team which can think on defense, the games between the two will soon began to recapitulate the evolution of modern football. One of the defensive tackles will begin it, as Link Lyman did with me so many years ago, by sliding off to avoid blockers. The attacking quarterback will take only so much of this, and then he will think of a way to hang up that tackle, by reassigning his blockers.

As he grows smarter, the quarterback will learn how to cope with a zone defense against his receivers one week, and a man-for-man setup the next. He will try to flood a zone to put too much weight on one man, in the first case. He will begin crisscrossing his receivers in the second case, in hopes of confusing the defense and forcing a costly switch in the assignments. And so it will go, as football history has gone, with variations born by the minute.

Attack has been curbed only to the extent of throwing out freaks which unquestionably demanded more than reasonable acuity by the defense. How? Well, for one, the practice of making tackles and guards and even the center eligible for pass receiving by last-second shifts which placed such a player on either end of the line.

Such stunts got out of hand, and could hardly be supervised by the referee. With spreads, and the man-in-motion off the T, it became impossible for an official to watch continually for eligible and ineligible pass receivers, and rhubarbs sprouted from week to week.

Here is an example of the type of stuff which could be so confusing. Mel Hein, Giants center, was made eligible for a pass in a game with the Bears. We did this by lining up in an unbalanced formation, with a lone end to the left of Hein. Harry Newman acted as T quarterback, behind Hein. Just before he signaled for the snap, one of our backs moved into the line and the left end dropped off a yard, leaving Hein the outside man. Newman took the ball and immediately passed it back between Hein's legs. George Musso, Bears guard, slanted in to grab Newman. He actually shook Harry, looking for the ball. Meanwhile Mel walked through two opposing halfbacks and had gone about twenty yards downfield before Carl Brumbaugh, playing safety, got suspicious, and took out after Hein to drop him near the goal.

Plays such as that brought about the rule that men intended to work on the ends of the line must be designated in advance as ends, no matter what their normal position might be.

The attack used to be permitted a great deal more leeway on screen passes than is the custom now. In the old days, linemen didn't stay put, as required, until the ball was thrown, but pelted downfield to knock somebody over. That rule is a difficult one to enforce strictly, and teams still take advantage now and then, but gross violations are no longer accepted by the officials.

That reminds me of a story about George Halas, coach of the Bears. We worked a screen pass on his team which was probably illegal. The pass went to huge Cal Hubbard, a tackle playing end. Our linemen would hike out at the snap, and not wait for the throw, to clear the deck for Hubbard. Cal made a number of good gains in one game against the Bears, and the next time we played, Halas presented a diagram of the play to the referee, Jim Durfee.

Halas stated: "This play is illegal and they can't use it."

I asked Durfee if I might see the diagram. Halas had it laid out almost exactly, and I was in for some tall talking.

I began: "Jim, Mr. Halas has this drawn out this way. We don't run it exactly that way. We run it legal."

Durfee didn't look too favorable, and I added: "Furthermore, Jim, you've officiated enough games to know whether we run a play legal or not, without looking at a diagram."

That did it. Durfee snapped: "I sure have. Get away from me, Halas."

Durfee was a colorful official of the old time, who attained quite a reputation for rule-of-thumb decisions such as he gave Halas.

One game in Pittsburgh the passer for the Steelers threw the ball away after he was tackled.

With time out, I walked across the field to Durfee and asked: "That was intentional grounding, wasn't it, Jim?"

He answered quite sincerely: "Now, Steve, I was standing right there looking that boy right in the eye, and that boy didn't have any intention of grounding that pass."

Gus Dorais told me one of the best of the Durfee stories. Gus played for Massillon in the traditional game in neighboring Canton, in Ohio. These cities waged one of the earliest and most celebrated rivalries of football. Canton was ahead with two minutes to go, when Dorais threw a pass to a receiver in the end zone. As the latter caught it, the crowd flooded into the zone and surrounded him. When the fans stepped back, the receiver had no ball and no jersey.

The Massillon players demanded a touchdown call by Durfee, but old Jim knew it was no place for a decision unfavorable to that home-town crowd on the field. He ran for the nearest gate, and yelled: "See me in the hotel and I'll give you my decision!"

Officials today are better trained, but no smarter than old Jim, who had an answer to handle any problem. Seriously, I have always had the highest respect for the work done so conscientiously by our officials.

They have to watch twenty-two men thrown into action at the one instant, and therefore have one of the hardest games to run. They are under pressure at all times, and often work in difficult circumstances.

I have always tried to get along with officials, and I avoid riding them. I feel that no official ever scored a point against me, and that, while a referee or one of his gang can miss a play now and then, he doesn't muff nearly so many as the players in their execution of plays. Therefore, I concentrate on players, not officials, who can neither win nor lose for me.

Getting back to offense, I have tried to show how it boils down mechanically to timing in the basic plays, and then ingenuity in working out variations for special situations.

After that, there are two more elements to be considered, the surprise and the gamble.

The surprise, of course, involves deception in either over-all plans for the game or play-by-play as the action happens. There is nothing more important in football than that one costly moment of doubt the defense must have against a smartly trained attack. Trifling hesitation by a defense man before he dares commit himself is all the smart and alert running back or pass catcher needs to get one fatal step on the fellow guarding him.

One of the poignant movies we have in our library could be entitled "The Surprise Which Didn't Work." The film covers our 10–0 loss to the Browns in the Polo Grounds in 1951. We counted on getting the draw on Cleveland on our first play from scrimmage, on a pass from Chuck Conerly to Bosh Pritchard. The play worked perfectly—up to a point. Pritchard, left half in the T, faked perfectly to reach the open behind Hal Herring of the Browns. At that stage in the movies I can see a touchdown, or a very long gain. But a few frames later the dream vanishes, because Conerly, with an ailing shoulder, did not lead Pritchard, and threw a ball that hung.

We wanted the first score because that is often conclusive in a game between two sound, well-matched teams. The one which gets the jump has the assurance to sit on the lead, meanwhile jabbing the other fellow into mistakes, which can lead to more scoring.

We missed, but the Browns didn't. Dub Jones scored on their touchdown chance, and they had command of the game. Thereafter, we couldn't prevent Ford, Willis, and Kissell from rushing Conerly often enough to ruin his passing at critical points. The team which scored first won, which is so often the case between even opponents.

We registered several strategic surprises in 1950 when I added the A to the T. The Cardinals, under Curly Lambeau, had beaten us in Chicago with a very tough defense against the T. I decided to go back to A formation for the return match in New York. At least half the boys on the Cards defense had never seen the A, and Lambeau had to stay in his T defense. We gained 600 yards, scored over fifty points, and stayed in the title running.

After the game Lambeau complained: "Why didn't you save that for the Eagles next week? Why did you have to pull it on me?"

I understood he didn't like to look bad—nobody does. But I thought to myself that he hadn't been at all considerate of me with his rugged and winning T defense three weeks before. I did not say that, however, with regard for Lambeau's sort of stormy mood of the moment. Curly had transferred from Green Bay to the Cardinals and was having a difficult time with that former championship club. The following year, Lambeau resigned.

I went back to the T against the Eagles, but counted on the A for the game with the New York Yanks. However, they had scouted the A and would have defenses set up to meet it. Therefore, I ran the A from right to left against them, instead of left to right, as they had seen it against the Cardinals. Before Red Strader, coach, could adjust his defenses, we had two touchdowns and were away on another fifty-point romp.

I guess there is nothing which galls more than a penalty which cancels a nicely played surprise. We had such a case in 1950, in the conference play-off with the Browns in the frozen-field game in Cleveland. It was our most costly penalty in years, because it lost our crack at the title. They led 3–0, with the Giants on their four-yard line. This was the chance—the only chance either side had to score a touchdown—and I thought I had the play to do it.

This was a pass from Conerly to Bob McChesney, end. However, I made a bad move before the play started. I subbed Kelly Mote at end, because he could throw a hard block, if that were needed, and he was a sure-handed receiver, who would provide Conerly with another target in case McChesney were knocked down or covered too closely. I was trying to get all the percentage I could on the play. My master-minding backfired. McChesney caught the pass wide open. He fooled the Browns completely. But Mote had been offside, and the play was dead. Mote had not been needed for any purpose, but he ruined the play. I didn't blame him. He was doing his best in a moment of high tension. Maybe he had tried to anticipate the snap by a fraction of a second, maybe the center had delayed a fraction. It didn't matter how it happened when it was over; it was just one of those breaks which no one can predict or prevent. We didn't have another chance like that, and the Browns won, 8–3.

The Giants won by 14–7 from the Redskins in Washington in 1943, although we didn't make a first down all day. We didn't have to, because we got the jump on them. When the game opened, it seemed sure to rain, and I instructed Tuffy Leemans to try for a touchdown pass as soon as he got the ball.

No one ever followed orders better. On the first play Tuffy connected with Will Walls for a touchdown. Soon after, O'Neale Adams intercepted a pass by Dick Poillon, and scored another. That was not luck; we had gambled on stealing a favorite play of the Redskins, a wide flat pass, and had our ends play inside their ends. Sam Baugh had a great day passing in the rain, but we held him to one touchdown.

We threw only the one pass and didn't make a first down, but our opening surprise play gave us the bulge.

Gambling is a subject which fascinates fans. They like it. So do I. But I hope they wouldn't go against a game rigged 60–40 for the house. I don't like to gamble, either, if I can't see something close to an even break on the odds. Nevertheless, a small percentage of my correspondents through the years demand suicide gambles from me. They urge me to try to hold the ball on fourth down anywhere on the field, no matter what the circumstances. They also want to see lots of long passes thrown, without regard to the caliber of defense we face from game to game. Well, that's not gambling to me. That's hara-kiri.

I think these few fans are like the people who love to see a free swinger in the boxing ring, a fellow who rushes in with little wariness and small respect for his opponent, and who is generally carried out cold. He may put on a good show for a short while, but he is not going to win much more than beans money for his efforts.

It's the same in football. The team which wades in taking reckless chances is bound to be tagged on the chin. It's a scientific game, and not a slugging match.

That is seen clearly in any game in which both teams are in the running for the title. There is a lot of fencing in those games, because neither side can risk giving anything away. Games are won as much on the other fellow's mistakes as on your own ability, and the bad errors are put up on the scoreboard.

I have tried to hold the ball on fourth down in all sorts of setups, but never without a reason. We lost a game to the Rams in 1945 when I ordered a rush instead of a kick with one to go, on fourth down on our forty-five. We didn't make it, and the Rams, who then represented Cleveland, took over to score the winner in a 21–17 game. I tried to hold the ball because I could not match the substitutes Adam Walsh, Rams coach, had and my regulars were fading fast in that fourth period. I had to gamble they could keep the ball away from the Rams, who went on to win the world title that year.

Several times, in games already cited which were important in the race, notably against the Redskins and the Browns, the Giants were praised for scoring a touchdown with three to go on fourth down, when a cinch field goal would have tied. I took those gambles only because I had reasonable expectancy of getting the ball once more if we had lost it at the goal.

Sound judgment in football is based on a knowledge of the calculated risks in any situation; going heavily against the percentage as a habit is simply sucker stuff.

One more point I would like to insert here is the Giants' practice of kicking off, rather than receiving, when the opening toss is won. That has been the subject of more letters, both caustic and thoughtful, than anything we have done in recent years. Fans rightly want to know why I, in effect, give away the ball at the start, and let the other fellows have first chance to score.

I do it because I expect the Giants to score first through that stratagem, and in one recent season we did get the first touchdown or field goal in every game at the Polo Grounds within five minutes, although we kicked off in each.

Through the years I have learned that almost every team is likely to have a degree of tenseness in the first few minutes, which tends to cause jittery handling of the ball. I want the other side to have the ball in that nervous period. I want them to have the responsibility, and my side to have the chance of recovering a fumble or intercepting a poorly thrown pass.

Meanwhile, the Giants can get rid of their nervousness in the best way possible, by plowing in vigorously and hitting the other fellows.

When I give up the ball at the kickoff I naturally expect my defense to hold the other side down there near their goal, and I generally have the boys who can do that. Then, on a return kick, I am starting my first attack around our forty or at mid-field, instead of down inside our twenty.

Now for the various formations. The T has been a blessing to lighter boys, who would not have much chance in the hard-hitting blocking of the single wing. Boys who are not heavyweights but who have speed above the average shine in the T. Also, the system offered the opportunity to boys who were not fast and not hard runners, but who could pass well and learn to fake with the ball, to become quarterbacks. George Ratterman, Paul Christman, and Tommy Thompson are several who come to mind.

When I played, back in the twenties, the great man was Bronko Nagurski, a fullback with such power and driving force that massed defense had no better than an even chance to stop his battering-ram plunges for first down.

With the T, and its man-in-motion, which spread defenses and put lighter men out on the flank where they had running room, fellows such as Bosh Pritchard, Buddy Young, Dick Todd, and George McAfee became backfield stars. These speedy but light-side players would not have been considered for the old game I knew, the game of brute force.

The same applies to ends who were too light to apply

the rugged blocks of single wing. In the T these men were spread off from center, where they could maneuver. Jim Benton, Hugh Taylor, Ken Kavanaugh, Mac Speedie, Dante Lavelli were among those who prospered in that fashion. Don Hutson, greatest of all the ends, was in single-wing formation with the Packers, but Curly Lambeau used him in T style, set out clear so that he had the space to outfox blockers.

Speed, rather than power, became increasingly important as the T developed, and the T even allowed the use of lighter linemen, because of the brush block, which requires an opponent to be held only momentarily and not blasted off his feet. Danny Fortmann, a 185-pound guard, was one of the best draft picks George Halas ever made. Fortmann was No. 30 on the Bears' list, but he ranks among their all-time guards for effectiveness.

The T allowed boys to play center who would never have been able to snap from single wing, because with the hand-back pass a T center may keep his head up to block his man.

The salient points of the T are the chance it offers for deception, and its facility in spreading defenses.

The ball on almost every play can be well hidden as the quarterback turns his back from center, if he keeps elbows close to the body and executes fast-hitting plays with polished fakery. You can develop ball-handling magicians in the system. Bob Waterfield, of the Rams, is probably beyond compare. When he first became a star with the grand young team Danny Reeves assembled to win the world title for Cleveland in 1945, Waterfield actually walked around our right flank to a touchdown in the Polo Grounds while our defense pounced on decoy backs. Bob, with his unusually long, slender fingers, held the ball lengthwise against the brown of his pants, and casually strolled over the goal. Even in our movies of the game, it was difficult at first to believe Waterfield had kept the ball.

When he hides the ball, the quarterback holds the defense stationary for that vital moment of hesitation until his play forms. Then, with his lightning-quick openers, his pitchouts, and passing off of fakes, he can count on getting a step on the defense. That slim advantage is the most he can expect, but often it is enough.

The T, through the man-in-motion, took the stranglehold off offense, by loosening the defense. The T, with its brush blocks, allows men to slip their first contacts and run downfield in time for secondary blocks to help the ball-carrier or receiver. If a man pops loose in the T, he often has a good chance to go all the way.

The gimmick which revived the T, which, by the way, was merely a stodgy set formation in old times, was the man-in-motion. Before that, the T could be squeezed to death by pressure from the flanks inward, as in the action of a nutcracker. When the man-in-motion was sprung wide, the defense still could squeeze what was left, but the floating man-in-motion could receive passes all day long. The defense had to realign to protect against the outrider, and thereby restored competence to the T's line attack.

The Bears started the man-in-motion, with Red Grange as the original. Grange missed a signal one day and ran wide before the ball was snapped. Ralph Jones, coach, stopped Red's apologies and asked him to do it again.

Jones had Grange repeat it again and again. He was a keen student of the game, and caught the significance of Grange's "mistake" immediately, because he had noted the defense shifting as soon as Grange took off, before the ball was snapped.

The man-in-motion always was legal; no one thought

of it until Grange stumbled on it and Jones perceived its value.

That's the way many football plays are devised, by accident. It can happen in a game, or while the coach is running scrimmage. A kid does something a little different which gives the coach an idea, and he gets to work to polish up a play based on his observation.

The reaction of the defense is the test of any play. All plays look great on paper, because on paper a coach always has the defense under control. He can place those opposing eleven men wherever he pleases. But in action, he may think he had only a bad dream, because he cannot keep the defense where he would like it. Those boys cross him up every time.

Today's single wing does not resemble the formation I played back in the twenties, any more than the modern T resembles the T without man-in-motion.

The single wing now demands speed and mobility equally with the T. No matter what formation you play, you have got to match speed for speed, as well as block with block, and tackle with tackle.

However, the demands on personnel vary from the T in the single wing. Driving runners are needed, boys who can hit for a few extra yards when first tackled, as well as the outside-type runner of the T. Of course there must be a good ball-handler in the backfield—that goes for every system. Ends must be able to block as well as the tackles and guards, so as to double-team an opposing tackle. Linemen must be able to handle blocking on the trap play, in which an opposing lineman is suckered across the line to be eliminated by a block on his flank. The quarterback in single wing is primarily a blocker, who must also be able to catch passes well. The right half, located wide on the wing, near the end, must be very fast and must be able to block and catch.

The fullback has to handle the ball, spin, and drive, as well as block. The left half must be a superior ball-handler and passer and a blocker.

The left halfback in the single wing has a considerable advantage over the T quarterback in passing. The left half does not have to turn his back to the line to retreat for the pass. He is already back there, with full view of the downfield defense situation and eligible receivers at all times. Sam Baugh, the deadliest passer in football history from the single wing, lost some of his effectiveness when the Redskins went to the T, and in emergencies Baugh would go into an improvised double-wing attack for passing.

If the boy is a hard runner as well as an exceptional passer, the optional play by the single-wing passer is the most dangerous single stratagem in football. A boy such as Charlie Trippi, or Frank Filchock, or Joe Geri illustrates the point in mind.

In this play, the man with the ball has the defense at his mercy. They must commit themselves when the play is well done. When the runner begins his slide to right or left, he watches the defense keenly. If they come in to tackle, he can throw over their heads. If they go back to guard against the pass, he most likely will find a hole where he can run. This is one of the most exciting plays of the game.

The single wing, in over-all strategy, is designed to control the ball. It is not founded chiefly on surprise and deception, as is the T, but on power blocking, which is a much more constant quantity. Gains normally are shorter in single wing than in T, but more regular. It is not exceptional to see a single-wing team hold the ball for five or six minutes while staging one drive. This prolonged possession often exerts terrific nervous pressure on the other team, in the already strained atmosphere of action and the passing of precious minutes.

The double-wing system, as a regular attacking formation, requires a passing quarterback, halfbacks who can throw or receive on reverse passes, and a big spinning fullback who can drive and hand off.

However, the double wing nowadays is generally used as a diversion to exert passing pressure, for which it is best suited. With backs on both wings, it is possible to get four men, two backs and two ends, downfield more rapidly than in any other formation, especially from spreads. It is possible to use five receivers if the passer is deep so that he does not require extra blocking.

The fifth receiver, generally the fullback, can be a touchdown menace on a screen pass, when he fakes a block and slides off into the flat behind charging tackles and ends.

Jimmy Phelan, coach of the New York Yanks in 1951, did a remarkable job with limited material in the spread double wing. He started with a former T quarterback, Bob Celeri, who was handicapped in that position by his short stature. But as a deep, standback passer, Phelan put Celeri's powerful arm to most advantageous use. Celeri, ten yards back of the line, with the option of dropping back ten more, made it virtually impossible for rushing linemen to put pressure on him before he found a target. Phelan had just enough running to keep the defense honest. He was not a winner, but he was able to play extremely close, exciting games because of his selection of the most suitable system for the talents of his squad. Had he stayed in the T, it would have been almost impossible for him to achieve as much.

I have known Phelan since he was coach at Missouri and I was at college. Jimmy played pro football at Toledo following his discharge from the army after the first war, and I have seen his teams, always smartly coached, in his later years with the colleges. Phelan was a fiery leader as Notre Dame quarterback, and he carried that inspirational quality with him into coaching.

For balance, however, the double wing must have the dauntless type of old-fashioned fullback who can blast through tacklers. Ernie Nevers, the star of Warner's Stanford double wing, made that system work in the NFL because of his own ability. The Cardinals ran two sets of backs in practice, but in the game Nevers worked with both. Without him, the formation lacked its bite.

I mentioned split lines before. Spreading the men in that way, out of shoulder-to-shoulder formation so that there is spacing between them, forces the defensive linemen to cover more territory. Our spread in A formation, for instance, is of the width ten men would occupy in tight alignment. The defense has to cover that spread with five, six, or seven men. That is not only difficult but costly, and, if the line is reinforced, naturally the passing has a higher percentage in its favor.

Splits offer a fast back more chance to pop through on quick openers, afford improved blocking angles on defensive men, and provide more room to maneuver to hold a hole open.

Why doesn't the split let defense men come in easier? It would, if blocking were not set up to take advantage of their position, which is spread also. The protective pocket for the passer is in the form of a wedge so that rushers are forced outside. If linemen, from their spread, charge hard, the screen pass is the answer. Above all, the blocking angles permit the offense men to keep their bodies between the defense and the ball. A man coming straight in on a blocker often can get by on either side with the use of his hands. But if he is coming up on one side, he does not have a choice of direction, and the blocker finds it possible to maintain a shield by turning with the charge.

I had the idea for the A formation from the first time I saw Link Lyman slide off from the customary tackle position. He showed me what line splits could achieve.

I worked out the formation first in 1935 but did not use it until 1937, against the Redskins in Washington. When we first showed it, the Redskins defense men yelled: "Look out for the double wing!" But it was something they had never seen and they couldn't stop it. Leemans gained seventy-five yards in the first ten minutes and there is no telling what he would have totaled, if he hadn't been injured.

We finished second in '37 and went with the A all the way in '38 to win the world title by defeating Green Bay 23–17. But I am not going to claim the A did it all—we had a bunch of mighty good players, who would have been stars in any formation.

My theory behind the A was this: I wanted to spread without losing concentrated attacking power, and yet keep the defense scattered along a wide front so that it could not jam in on us at any point.

To do this I hit on the idea of deploying my line strong to one side, and my backs strong to the other side. So far as I know this was an original formation.

In the A, the line shows four men to the right of center and two to the left. But in the backfield the weight is to the left of center, with the wingback out on the left flank. The formation can be run in the other direction, with line strong to the left and backs heavy on the right. The

A exaggerates the effect of a split line, to carry the spread into the backfield.

When first introduced, we did not use the man-in-motion before the snap, but that factor was soon developed for Ward Cuff. From wingback he moved toward the slot between left half and fullback, with the timing to arrive there as the left half spun to make his fakes or hand offs. This reverse alone made Cuff one of the great backs of football.

I believe we showed spectacular proof of the running power of the A in 1943 and 1944, when Bill Paschal, a boy who had no college training, was able to lead the league in rushing for two straight years in my own formation. In 1950 the Giants were team leaders at ground-gaining, and in 1951 they had the individual leader in Eddie Price, with the A formation largely responsible.

When we first experimented with the A we had used the standard single wing, and in practice we called my new system A and the single wing B. After noting the possibilities the new formation opened up, we thought it should rightly head the alphabet as A, and we forgot about B and the other twenty-four letters as well.

We felt that in A formation, with the left halfback handling the ball as he does, and with man-in-motion, we had captured the essentials of the T, while retaining the power blocking of the single wing. Then too, we found that, while keeping our splits, we shift very easily into double wing, or Double A, as the writers call it, by moving our fullback on to the open wing.

Also, in the A we can quick-kick at any time, which is not possible in the T, and which is a handicap of that formation. I believe the A, since 1937, has run into more different defenses than any other system in football. Some, to my sorrow, were unexpectedly successful but never remained so.

As for deception, we have it in a measure equal to the T with our left halfback handling the ball as he does, that is, with synchronized faking possible by two backs at the one instant. I don't think any one play ever received more publicity as the "perfect play" than did Bill Paschal's fifty-three-yard quick-opener trap touchdown run against the Redskins in 1943. Not a hand was laid on Paschal for fifty-three yards.

I had to diagram this play for newspaper and syndicate use and for information of writers literally hundreds of times. It was distributed nationally by the news outlets. Here it is again:

Emery Nix was left half, and Dave Brown the wingback. Brown faked his end-run reverse so well that he drew off the Redskins' secondary. Meanwhile, Paschal roared through the quick-opener hole over guard after their guard had been trapped. Brown faked his job so well that I thought he had the ball and followed him, until I caught Paschal out of the corner of my eye when he was about the ten-yard line. Sam Baugh, safety man, had been pulled just far enough out of position by Brown so that he could not recover to bother Paschal.

All Bill had to do was sprint—along the shortest distance to the touchdown, a straight line—to win the game.

In all fairness to a great quarterback, I must present Baugh's explanation of the play here. The way he tells it, he gives us credit for strategic surprise, and not tactical surprise in the ball-handling. I quote Baugh from a clip of an interview at the time:

"I expected a pass, particularly since Brown, a fast runner and a fresh man, had just been put in there. I wasn't fooled by the ball-handling, but was going over on pass defense assignment, to pick up either the end or the wingback. Just you tell me any other losing club which wouldn't have passed with less than five minutes to go and still in their territory."

At least we can all agree the play was a surprise, from whatever angle.

A while back I noted the trend to the use of two systems by the one team, and I believe the ultimate in attack will be attained when a club is able to shift from formation to formation, from play to play.

But that depends on personnel, and I have not been able to switch from A to T as a regular thing, because I have not had the interchangeable men. As a stunt, I did have three plays run in sequence from three different formations once in 1951. We started with double wing to complete a pass, went into A to gain running, and then, from T, scored on a quarterback sneak.

It is easy for us to go into double wing from either A or T on a shift before the ball is snapped. But not from T to A or vice versa, because of the lack of a back who has the running ability for the T and the blocking power for the A. In changing from T to A, I must pull Joe Sulaitis, running guard, out of the T, install him as blocking quarterback in the A, and sub a lineman in the A line in place of a back from the T. Conversely, on a move from A to T, Sulaitis moves into the line to force one man out, and a new T back must come in. All this isn't as simple as it sounds!

You can readily see that my problem would be solved, if I had that one back who could play halfback or fullback in the T, and blocking back in the A. And that's like having brains, good looks, and money all at once. When we made our draft picks for 1952 we selected Frank Gifford, of the University of Southern California, not only because he had been named All-America halfback by the American Coaches Association, but because he was one of the most versatile halfbacks to come up in many years. He showed hard-running ability, accurate passing, strong blocking, excellent place-kicking, and also superior quality on defense! In addition, he had played well in the T and in the single wing! He worked sixty minutes in two bowl games! You find all-around players of quality such as Gifford very rarely nowadays.

I planned, through Gifford's versatility, to attempt to work the switch from formation to formation from play to play.

That was the dream—to go from A to T to double wing to southwest spread from play to play. With that dream realized, I could put unprecedented pressure on defenses, particularly since many teams cannot handle several formations without changing personnel. Whether the Giants or some other team achieves it first, it is the coming thing in football.

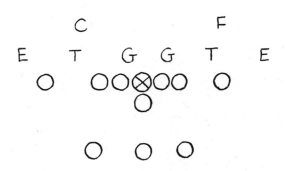

T Formation

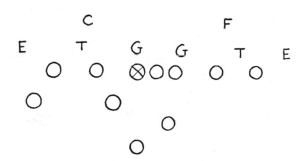

The Owen A Formation

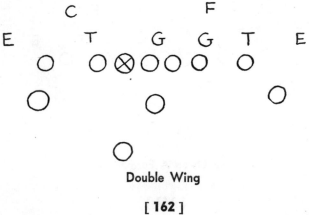

Single Wing

Double Wing

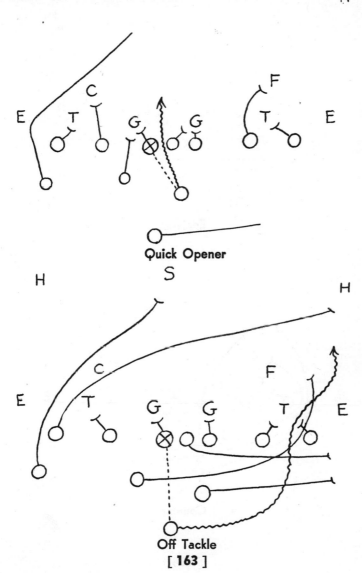

Quick Opener

Off Tackle

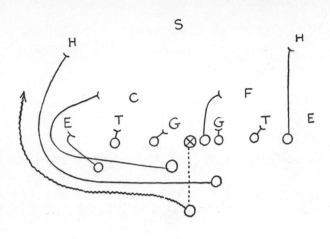

End Run

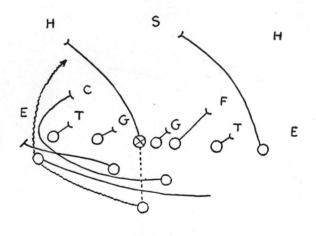

Counter

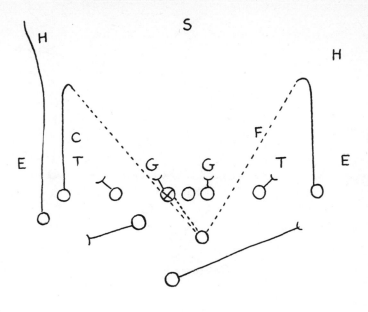

Hook Pass

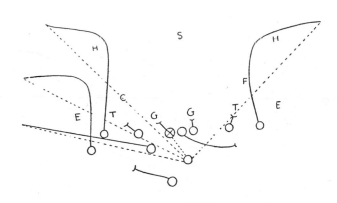

Fan Pass

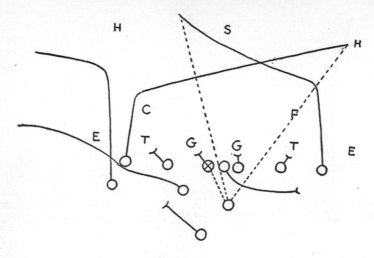

Crossover Pass

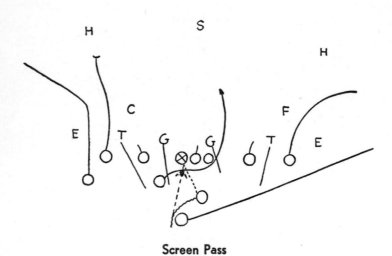

Screen Pass

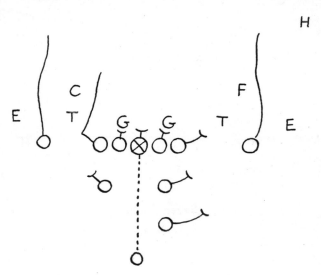

Punt Formation

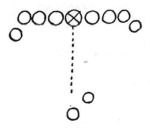

Place-Kick Formation

O   O   O

O
E   O   OO⊗OO   O   E
  T G C G T
       F

H   H

S

Seven Diamond

O   O   O

O
E   O   OO⊗OO   O
  T G C G T   E
  H   H

H   H

Seven Box

BASIC DEFENSE FORMATIONS

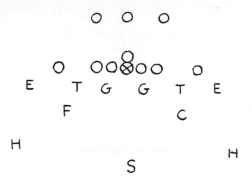

6–2–3 Defense

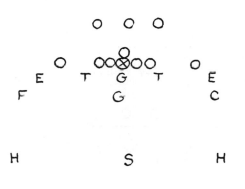

5–3–3 Defense

BASIC DEFENSE VARIATIONS

6–1–4 Variation

6–3–2 Variation

5–1–5 Variation

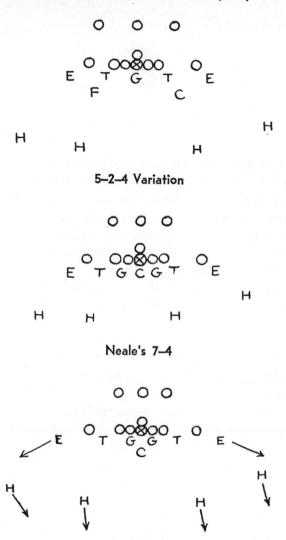

5–2–4 Variation

Neale's 7–4

Owen's "Umbrella"

8

~~~~~~~~~~~~

I LIKE TO SET UP DEFENSES. DEFENSE IS HALF OF THE GAME, and neglecting it is just plain foolish. Mistakes cost you close games to teams which, because of good defense, can take advantage of errors. It's the same in any sport.

There were two conspicuous examples in baseball, for instance, in recent years. When the Boston Red Sox had Ted Williams and tremendous batting power, they couldn't quite beat down the Yankees, a sound all-around club with a great center line of defense. (Catching, pitching, second-base combination, and center fielder.) The Brooklyn Dodgers of 1951 were another team with a terrific attack, but they were defeated by the Giants, who had the pitching and the fielding to reduce errors in their great stretch drive.

I like to run my football team with just as much attention to defense as offense. I never try to present a game to the other club; they must earn it. When I am ahead, I think it is only fair that the other fellow should come to me and take the chances, because I have to do that when I am behind. Once again, I would much rather win by 3–0 than lose by 38–36.

I don't want to worry whether I can score 30 to 40 points, while secretly feeling my team figures to give away that many. A loose club puts the coach on the acid side.

He goes around ready to bite man or beast. I know. I had an outfit on those lines in 1948. We scored more points than any Giant team in history—and allowed more. We won four, lost eight, which is one of the best ways for a coach to join the unemployed.

Maybe I was lucky, but I wasn't fired. About the only satisfaction I got that season came verbally, not in action. Several of my friends among the newspapermen had the habit of referring to me with a pleasant sneer as a "defensive" coach, and demanding that the Giants score more points.

One of our games in the Polo Grounds resulted in a 52–37 win for the Los Angeles Rams. As I sat by my locker wondering why fate had skipped over me in allotting high-quality defensive halfbacks, the writers came in. I had the laugh on them for once. I commented: "Fellows, it's a darned good thing I am such a great defensive coach. If I weren't they never would have been able to get the Rams' points up on that scoreboard today."

Defense, just like offense, gets down to the men who play the game. If they know their business, the coach looks good; and if they don't, there isn't much he can do about it. In 1943 the Bears scored fifty-six points on the Giants. Hunk Anderson was running the team while George Halas was in the Navy, and Hunk kept the pressure on for sixty minutes to enable Sid Luckman to set an all-time record of seven touchdown passes. Our halfbacks had no chance to stop the slaughter, because they couldn't run as fast as the Chicago receivers.

We met the Bears next in 1946, and they couldn't score a point. We beat them 14–0. The difference between the two games was in our personnel. We had the right men three years later.

When a coach has the men, there is no more mystery to

defense than there is to offense. Defense is based on two standard formations, the 6-2-3, and the 5-3-3. All else is "variations." Top football men learn to assume this fact, depending on the type of attack set against them.

Earl Blaik, with his great Army teams, and Bob Neyland, with his rugged Tennessee clubs, used the 6-2-3 most of the time, with slight variations. It has been used successfully by many coaches without switching very often into anything else. It's a sort of "all-purpose" formation.

The 5-3-3 is the basic defense of the Cleveland Browns, and it has served through the years to make the Pittsburgh Steelers always a tough team to score on. It's like being in the center of town, where everything you need is within reach.

One more fundamental defense alignment may be added to the 6-2-3 and the 5-3-3, but not for general use. This system is the 7-4 devised by Greasy Neale, and used almost exclusively by his champion Philadelphia Eagles. However, this formation can be handled only by experts and is a risky one for the average team.

But none will work without adequate personnel, and, if a coach can get a sure-fire safety man, half his worries about long-distance touchdowns are over. One of my favorite specialists on that back line of defense was Hank Soar, who has been an umpire in the American League since 1949.

Soar always was cool and poised, as if he were strolling down the avenue on Easter Sunday. This attitude sometimes worked on my nerves. In the heat of battle, you could swear it was indifference. During one game we had a slim lead on the Redskins with a few minutes to go, and Sammy Baugh was winding up and throwing the ball almost every down to good receivers. Soar, on the other hand, looked the soul of unconcern and watched the clock, over his shoulder, as much as he did Baugh. It burned me up.

I couldn't stand it. I yelled: "Soar, you quit looking at that clock, and pay attention to Baugh. I'll tell you when the game is over."

He didn't turn my way, just waved his hand at me. "Why don't you quit bothering me out here," he yelled back. "Don't you see I'm busy?"

Soar's wits, as well as his wit, were always working. Baugh told me a story about him one time. "I thought I had him set up for a sure touchdown," Sammy recalled sadly, "and he had me set up for an interception instead." This was a great passer's tribute, as he discussed a game in which Hank's deception enabled us to nose out the Redskins for the eastern title.

"When we scored our touchdown," Baugh continued, "I noticed that Soar pulled away out of position. It wasn't his man and he was out of the play, but I filed away his move for future reference. When I got the chance, I called a pass which I felt sure would take advantage of his error. Soar was just kidding me. He smelled me out and was waiting for the pass. I sure had been taken."

Otto Schnellbacher, who became a Giant in 1950, is another shrewd safety man on Soar's type. Otto has often complimented an end who has faked him—when that end is not receiving.

Otto will say: "Sure glad the ball didn't come this way. You had me clear out of the play, pal."

Unless that end is a wise old bird he will rush back to his signal caller and rave about the touchdown he is sure to catch behind Schnellbacher. He is generally a cha-grined young man when he discovers that Otto fails to fall for his fake when a miss means a touchdown. Otto is likely to intercept instead, and that explains the secret of his threat as a steady interceptor.

Em Tunnell, another great defense man who keeps Schnellbacher company on our back line, told me a story about Otto and him, and their strategy on "Crazy Legs" Hirsch in the Pro Bowl game at Los Angeles in '52.

Hirsch was the most effective receiver in the league in '51. He scored seventeen touchdowns on passes and set a new all-time record of 1,495 yards with the Rams. He was the man Schnellbacher and Tunnell had to stop. How did they do it?

Tunnell relates: "Otto lined up with Hirsch every play. He looked him in the eye. He made sure to make Hirsch believe he was covering him. But Otto wasn't. He just wanted to get Hirsch off guard. Before the game he told me that he would draw Hirsch off and make him fake. But all the time I was to be running over, to come in behind Otto and catch Hirsch off his guard. That worked every time. Hirsch would pull a pretty fake on Otto and then sort of relax, and then he would have me on his neck when that ball arrived. He never did get on to it, and I wonder where he thought I came from."

Tunnell was the first Negro on the Giants, and he is a witty fellow as well as a talented player. He told us one day he had moved to a new house in his home town of Garrett Hill, Pennsylvania.

"It's twice as good a house as the old one," he boasted. "It's on the same street, but our old number was 24, and the new number is 48. That makes it twice as good, doesn't it?"

I will never forget the time Em thought he talked too much, though he didn't say a word.

Soon after he joined us, we played Philadelphia, and I

bawled him out between halves because I thought he should have intercepted a pass.

I could see the resentment beginning to flare in his eyes, and I figured he was about to snap at me. But Charley Porter, the famous Negro trainer who had been with the club since it was founded, apparently had the same size-up of Em's behavior.

Tunnell was sitting on the stool in front of his locker, and Porter came up behind him, clamped his hands on Em's shoulders, and said: "Boy, you just sit there and listen and you'll learn something." He listened.

After the game Em came to me. "Coach," he said, "I'd like to apologize for flaring up like I did at half time."

Defense was standardized until 1930. If a team didn't use the seven-diamond it used the seven-box. By that I mean there were seven men on the line, with the four backs arranged either in diamond formation or in a square, boxlike shape.

But I had thought of varying that routine alignment in 1929. The Giants were to play the Green Bay Packers in a game which was to decide the title, because they were unbeaten at the end with twelve won and one tied, while our record was twelve won, one lost, and one tied, with the lone defeat by the Packers, 20–6. We played one more game than they did, because the league in those times was on what you might call an informal schedule. Teams which couldn't put up a guarantee to stage home games had to hope they were attractive enough to be invited by the richer clubs. In 1929 there were twelve entries. One played eighteen games, two each played fourteen, thirteen, and ten games. The rest played twelve, eleven, nine, eight, and six games.

Curly Lambeau had the Packers running out of the Notre Dame box formation in '29, and I had felt for a long while that we would do better against them with a six-man line, with two backers-up, and three men back for passes. In brief, a 6-2-3, which was not used at the time. I pleaded with LeRoy Andrews, our coach, through the week before the game to try the six-man line. I tried to prove to him that they might make a little more on short gains running, but that we would have protection against breakaways and have more flexible coverage on passes.

Andrews finally agreed. Their first play came to me, at left tackle. They made three yards. Andrews was disgusted, threw out the six-man, and went to seven-diamond for the rest of the game. I don't think the coach had much faith in that six-man line.

In a few years, however, the six-man became common. The old seven-diamond and seven-box were passé, because of their vulnerability, and more so as passing and faking of receivers improved.

When I became coach I could put through my own ideas of defense, and I devised the five-man line in 1933. I believed it would contain the T better than anything then employed. I worked on it for two weeks before we met the Bears.

My idea was to maintain a line strong and flexible enough, with its three backers-up, to battle their running and cover them outside. At the same time I could have six men back against passes, by having those backers-up fade deep when the threat of a run was not present.

This was the first 5-3-3 defense, but it didn't last long. Bronko Nagurski wrecked it on his first play. I played Mel Hein and Bo Molenda as the outside backers-up, but had only one more man, Hank Reese, a guard, who was able to back up. I spotted him in the middle. On the first play the Bears sent the mighty Nagurski through center. My middle backer and the Bronko collided. Nagurski gained

[**178**]

six yards and Reese was carried off the field, out cold. That ended the five-man line until I got that middle guard in working order again for the next game.

We were the first to use the five-man as a regular thing. I worked it out on paper with Ox Da Grosa at a coaching clinic, and experimented with it in scrimmage immediately after. It took the T coaches several years to overcome it, and we won the division title in 1933–34–35.

We worked it in this way. Because the T was a balanced offense, with a tight-knit line, I felt I could play my tackles in a five-man defense closer than was normal, because of my three backers-up. The middle backer-up was on the head of the center, and the two wide backers covered inside or outside of the ends. The three backers-up gave me a second line of defense across the attacking area, and this trio could be moved readily, forward against running, backward against passes.

After the 6-2-3 and the 5-3-3 replaced the old box and diamond, many variations sprang from them, and defense gradually became as scientific and involved in maneuvers as offense.

I will try to explain how variations grew off these formations, but first, let's look over the setup of a defense.

There are defensive signal-callers, just as there are on offense. These are generally picked on the coach's observation in the regular classroom sessions, in which players study play-books and keep notebooks and are indoctrinated in the style of football to be followed.

The Giants were lucky in 1950 to have Bill Milner as their defensive signal-caller. When he went into service, we were fortunate to find that Arnie Weinmeister and Tom Landry, alternating, could do just as well in 1951.

This defense "quarterback" must be reasonably intelligent and absolutely quick-thinking. He must have a comprehensive grasp of the capabilities of his teammates and correctly interpret the circumstances of the moment. In that last-named category would be the score, the time remaining to play, the yardage and down, the known strength of the opposition for the situation at hand, and the physical condition of his men. This last factor is a subtle thing, but important. By physical condition I don't mean to imply the players are out of shape. I mean that some squads are not so well blessed in manpower as others, and because some players have had to play more minutes, they may not be so fresh as their opponents. The quarterback must concede they can't do as much as at the start.

The director of defense knows his fundamental strategy beforehand. He realizes he will be wiser, if his side is ahead, to let the attack make a short gain in order to reduce the chance of a long gain. His object then is to make the other fellows work hard for small return. If his side is trailing late in the game, then he has to take some risk of allowing a touchdown in order to put pressure on the attack to stop it, and regain the ball.

The defense "quarterback" gambles on his judgment. After that the individual players must alter their instructions by themselves, depending on the play. And when one man departs from the basic order, others, if they are alert, must take their cue and make their changes too.

Defense is a lot like several teams working together. I think I can explain that, by taking the left end, the left backer-up, and the left halfback of a formation. In brief, the left side of it.

The left end may crash or slide off on any play. If he crashes, the left backer-up must slant back at an angle to protect the hole. The left halfback then must hold back, and be wary against a deep play on his side, until the attack is committed, when he must come up very fast if the play is a short one.

If the left end drops off, the backer-up can go straight back, to play a zone against short passes, or charge up for a rush. The left halfback then need not worry about anything short, and is free to play zone against long passes, or man-for-man to take over the receiver covered either by the left end or the halfback on the right side.

The chain reaction extends to the safety position. We use two men there, and they form a team of their own. If the whole line, for instance, "reddogs," that is, smashes through to bother the passer, those two safety men will move up. With the pressure of all linemen operating on the passer, they know he isn't likely to have time to throw a long one, and, if he hands off, they can save yards by moving in on the rusher.

The back men talk it over from play to play, because football changes from play to play. Schnellbacher and Tunnell, for instance, thought out a special defense for the hook pass and worked it successfully against the Bears in New York. A hook pass is difficult to intercept, because it is thrown sharply to a receiver who turns to receive it, and because a defender who gets inside that receiver is inviting the risk of a long gain.

But Tunnell did it. He came up quickly on the inside of Ken Kavanaugh, caught the ball, and went fifty-seven yards for a touchdown. He came up on the inside so that he could break to the outside to avoid the linemen. He was able to make that daring play because of Schnellbacher, who went deep to cover Kavanaugh fully if Tunnell missed or if the Bears end tried a hook-and-go, in which the receiver tries not to break stride as he whirls for the ball. Our safety men worked it out so that if the chance came on Schnellbacher's side, Tunnell would have dropped back.

I think I have suggested, through these few examples of shifting tactics, that the value of a defense is chiefly in the speed, experience, alertness, and horse sense of the men on the field, and not in the coach. He can plot out the main strategy and talk for hours on the moves to be made if such and such a play should be sprung by the attack. But the coach can't go out and practice what he preaches; his men must. The coach isn't running the opposing attack, either; his men have to cope with that, and adjust to surprises on the moment. There are few sights in football that thrill a coach more than to see players make the blackboard "come alive" by meeting unexpected circumstances with quick thinking and physical alertness.

What the coach does, from his knowledge of a team, is to determine the opponent's strong suit, running or passing. If he is playing a team such as the championship Philadelphia Eagles, with the great running back Steve Van Buren, he knows he has to pack in line power to stop the running. He has to take a chance on shading his pass defense, because Van Buren is the grave menace, the surest shot for a touchdown on the Eagles. It doesn't do to let a Van Buren work into the open through a thin line, because that kind of power runner can be too much man for one halfback to handle. When he has running room, he is hard to check, and the trick is to keep him in heavy traffic on the line where he may be dragged down by two or three men.

But if the opponent is to be the champion Cleveland Browns, then the coach must consider passing first of all, because the combination of Otto Graham throwing, and Dub Jones, Dante Lavelli, and Mac Speedie receiving is by far their surest way of scoring. That means the coach has to give away a little against running, and make sure to cover those receivers. He has got to scheme to have more men covering passes than the Browns can shoot out to catch them, so that he may double-team the most dangerous receiver or pack another obstacle into a zone defense.

The coach doubtless will start with a 6-2-3 in his plans for the Eagles, or for a blasting single wing offense such as Jock Sutherland used to have with the Pittsburgh Steelers. He is likely to begin working with a 5-3-3 in thinking of the Browns, because that is the basic formation against passing.

But the coach knows he may have to switch on the field, if Philadelphia running is too strong for his 6-2-3, or Browns passing is too deadly for his 5-3-3. He instructs his team on possible variations.

He may have to swing into a 6-3-2 against the hard-running team. That is one of the toughest defenses to run against. But when the coach orders the 6-3-2, using an extra backer-up instead of a halfback, he knows he is inviting trouble from passes. However, he is right in doing so, because he knows the strongest opposing weapon, running, is sure to click, while the weaker one, passing, may misfire.

His switch against the Browns may put his defense into a 5-1-5, or a 6-1-4, depending on whether he wants to overshift as a means of double-teaming receivers, or to rush Graham. The Giants employed a 6-1-4 basic formation when they shut out the Browns in 1950, but on many plays this became a 4-1-6 in reality, when the ball was snapped, because the ends dropped off the line to afford extraordinary coverage on passes.

These defenses all work together. If a coach has the right men, his signal-caller can go from 5-3-3 to 6-2-3 to 6-3-2 to 6-1-4 to 5-1-5 on successive plays, although he hardly would have the occasion to do so against any one team. Circumstances dictate the changes. The shrewd and quick defensive signal-caller will recognize them.

This numerical presentation may make defense seem difficult, but the shifts really come almost instinctively to men who have practiced and played together for a long while.

For instance, if you are in 6-2-3 against the T, and a man goes in motion, you have to cover him either with a backer-up or a halfback. If the backer-up slants wide and deeper to do it, then you automatically have changed to a 6-1-4. If the halfback comes up to do it, then you have a virtual 6-3-2.

Of course, there are all sorts of personal maneuvers which do not change the formation, but which are annoying to the attack. This forces the offensive quarterback to call on his variations of the standard plays. At this point the chances of a mistake in your favor are highest, for pressure in any game is a major cause of blunders.

These last-minute moves into so-called variations are many. Linemen loop from one position to another. They vary the direction of their charge. They hold the charge one play, bust in on another. The end may float off into the flat one time, and bulldoze in at the passer on another. He may drop off to look for a hook pass, or he may simply stand where he is once in a while. That may be just the time the attack expects him to be drifting somewhere else, or counts on trapping him during a charge.

A spread attack, particularly from double wing, is likely to cause trouble with orthodox defenses. The spread attack spreads the defense too, and if the outside backers-up are wide, a good double-wing fullback can belt you up the middle. If the backers-up are tight, to take care of that fullback, the double wing can shoot four receivers—two ends and two wingbacks—right around the backers-up.

Then there are four men down for a pass and only two or three defenders to cover them. A special 6-1-4 might be the answer to the double wing, with the backer-up to move eye-to-eye with that fullback, and the ends to drop back on passes to help the backline.

I have purposely avoided bringing the 7-4 formation into a general appraisal of the more common setups, because the Neale device is intended only for specially trained personnel. It is too dangerous for indiscriminate use by the average team. It is known in the NFL as the "Philly defense," and few others care to risk it.

The 7-4 is a variation of the 6-1-4, but without the backer-up, which means that a breakthrough puts the ball-carrier in the open. That is why there is need for wise men on that seven-man line, fellows who are all good tacklers and who are not easily trapped to leave a gap. Neale had his four defense backs close to the line, no better than five yards back at times, which would immediately suggest a passing attack could get behind them. However, those seven linemen could put so much pressure on a passer that he seldom had time to wait until his ends could hike far downfield. The line alone had dozens of combinations in their defense. All seven might reddog in on the play one time, while some would hold, or even drop off at other times. One never knew, because the setup was ingenious and the tactics complicated.

Generally, big-league defenses are more balanced than in high school and college. They have to be, because the pros have too many outstanding players to ignore any. An overshift to stop running, if it is too pronounced, will open the way for a passing game which may not be of the best but which is adequate to take full advantage of an opening. The high-school and college clubs do not have a wealth of running and passing agents, as a rule, because of the competition in their fields.

They also have, in varying degree, men who are prone to make mistakes and who are likely to flub an opportunity. At the big-league level these men are not considered, because the twelve professional clubs have the pick of the best among all colleges throughout the country.

Just a word about the "umbrella" defense of the Giants. I would like to take it up because fans everywhere ask me about the term and I also have had letters from many parts of the country inquiring about it.

The nickname refers to the four backs, who roughly assume the shape of an open umbrella, with the two halfbacks shallow and wide and the two safety men deep and tight. Then, when we have a 6-1-4 formation there is the backer-up to suggest the handle of the bumbershoot.

The four men who originated this defense with us were Tom Landry and Harmon Rowe at halfbacks, and Schnellbacher and Tunnell at safety.

In general, it is the role of this umbrella to act as a sort of flexible basket and adjust itself to contain any attacking situation, by moving in on one side or dropping back on the other, but always as a unit, and never without interdependence.

To give another idea of variations on a basic formation, we use the umbrella most often in a 5-2-4, and work eight changes off it.

1. We can reddog the backers-up through the line, with the ends holding to protect the outside.

2. We can send in an end from one side and a backer-up from the other, with the backer-up on the end side sliding off to cover, and the end on the backer-up side dropping a few yards to protect the vacated area.

3. We can send all seven linemen and backers-up charging in.

4. With a man-in-motion, we can wheel the umbrella, to pull three men onto the strong side. We do that depending on the quality of the opposition.

5. We may play zone defense in the backfield, with backers-up dropping straight back watching out for hook passes.

6. We may play man-for-man in the backfield, with the backers-up covering the fullback and one flat. To give that a minor change-of-pace variation we sometimes slide an end out to cover the flat, in lieu of the backer-up.

7. We may go into a 5-1-5, with a combination of some men man-for-man and others in zone defense.

8. We may go into a 6-1-4, to shift rapidly into a 4-3-4, with a combination of man-for-man and zone, if a pass develops after the snap.

There may be many more individual reactions to situations which cannot be foreseen, but the above eight are all readily performed by our line and "umbrella" on signal.

A great deal of thought and practice goes into the fundamental defense a team is to use against a particular opponent, and then, when the kickoff comes, that defense may not be worth a nickel.

One time we played the Chicago Cardinals in the Polo Grounds. I thought we had a sure-fire defense to stop their T. The formation lasted exactly two plays. Why? Because Jimmy Conzelman, Cards coach, hadn't obliged me by thinking along my way.

I expected him to use Pat Harder or Ventan Yablonski, power runners, at fullback. Instead, he put Boris Dimancheff, a fast scooter, in the job. That changed their attack and our defense. Dimancheff, as man-in-motion, was an extraordinary threat to receive passes, and we had to overshift to take care of him.

Greasy Neale, however, gave me my hardest time, when he threw the split T at us in the Polo Grounds in 1950. It was the first time our men had ever run into a split T in the league, although most had seen it and a few had played against it in college.

We could just about hold off a touchdown for the better part of a period, with that split T steadily gaining. Bill Mackrides played quarterback and did a good job as a drifter who, because of that split line and spread defense, could take his option of running, passing, or pitching out wide.

When a defense can't handle a new offense, it is in the position of trying to put out a grass fire. If you don't stomp it out and get it under control fast, it's likely to mushroom on you. If the Eagles had made the touchdown in a hurry with that split T, our men might have felt the pressure and made mistakes trying to work out a new deployment.

As it was, we improvised a sketchy defense to hold off their first rush, and finally got organized so that Neale eventually was forced back into his close-formation T. We won, 7-3, in a bitter defensive battle.

Sometimes a coach can make a wrong calculation which may abruptly turn a win into a loss or radically change the trend of action. I can give two examples, one by Paul Brown and one by me, both wrong, in games Cleveland won by 14-13 and 8-3.

In the 14-13 affair in Cleveland in 1951, we were trailing, with about four minutes to go, and were in our territory, out of field goal range. A tricky, gusty headwind made passing almost impossible. We seemed to be stymied. Suddenly the Browns pulled men off the line. Ed Price and

Joe Scott made twenty-five yards in two runs. We had what we hoped for: a chance at a field goal, which, alas, just missed.

Brown explained later that he felt that we had to throw at that late stage, and, considering our poor position, regardless of the wind. I guess we would have, too, if he had waited one or two more plays to pull back his defense.

In the 8–3 play-off game of 1950, we were tied with the Browns at 3–3 with about four minutes to go. They were in their territory, and my aim was to keep them from field goal range. A frozen field made a long gain virtually impossible, except by a long and somewhat lucky pass. So I stripped my forward defense to flood passing areas with defenders. Graham did just what I had discounted. He ran up the middle far enough for Lou Groza to connect on a field goal. One team kicked the goal, the other didn't. Football life is like that.

The big thrill a coach has on defense comes through outwitting the super player, who makes him worry about a touchdown every minute he has the ball. Sammy Baugh, for instance, was the greatest passer we ever have seen, because of his great arm, his remarkable accuracy, and his uncanny faking. Baugh's fakes could tie halfbacks into pretzels. He would cock the ball, bring it down to drift off as if about to run, cock again, make a mock throw to one side, and shoot a touchdown to the other. The reaction of a halfback, even a good one, is to close in as soon as the passer takes down the ball. That's all right with ordinary passers, but not with Baugh. He was never committed until he was flat on the ground and the ball with him. I have seen Sam make bullet-like throws with his tremendous wrist action as he was nailed by a hard tackle and falling.

The trick for a safety in defending against a pass is to

hold his move until he sees that ball take to the air, and then move to defend as fast as he can. He will seldom be beat if he observes those two rules. He will often be beat if he is suckered into a stride or two toward the passer or if he hesitates before going with the ball.

The Giants had good luck with Baugh because, unlike most teams, we figured that it was a waste of manpower trying to rush him. He could throw too fast to be stopped. We didn't try to stop him. Instead, we covered his receivers closely to hold all gains to short ones and to tackle those receivers hard so that they had to pay full price for every yard.

Don Hutson, the greatest pass receiver we have had in the NFL, was another touchdown-maker who could not do much against us because we struck on his one flaw. We discovered that if we could make Hutson break to the outside when he got through the line, he found it difficult to cut back inside where he might run for a touchdown. Hutson, although he was setting all kinds of records at the time, did not score a touchdown on us in the first five games we played. We double-teamed him to keep him outside. Mel Hein, at backer-up, was the key man in turning Hutson toward the side line. Then the halfback would take over to make sure the great Packer end at best was limited to a medium gain on a fan pass to the side line.

The great men, such as a Hutson, a Baugh, or a Van Buren, to include receiver, passer, and runner, are the ones who can beat any defense. That kind of fellow is a little better than the game, and if he has a good squad with him, the chances are he will be the difference in winning the game. As you can see, individual greatness, backed by a reasonably good team, will not be denied.

The Giants played pretty good all-around ball in 1951, and we had a chance for the title. I believe we lost the championship race to Cleveland because of two tackles: two tackles we failed to make on the same man—Dub Jones. In his greatest season, Jones was a terror. He was truly an outstanding player, and to me he was the difference between Cleveland and New York.

Jones ran through our team to score the first touchdown in our 14–13 defeat in Cleveland. Then at New York he took a screen pass for sixty-five yards to get the jump on us and change the game, in our 10–0 loss to the Browns. At least three of our crack defense men had clear shots at Jones the first time. John Cannady, our star backer-up, hit Jones behind the line the second time and did not stop him. Dub then was able to outmaneuver four of our fast and experienced defenders to score.

Now, I know our men are good on defense, as good as you will find. So when Jones was able to get away from them twice in critical games, I had to give the credit to him for two great plays.

Of course, whenever I run off the movies of those games I can second-guess how the two tackles could have been made. I can almost see them being made as the reel unwinds. I mutter to myself, "We got him this time sure!" But that Jones always gets through. Then I always end up with added respect for William A. Jones. He hurt us, but it's fellows like him who keep this game from being too cut and dried.

9

~~~~~~~~~~

I STEPPED INTO THE GIANTS' DOWNTOWN OFFICE ONE DAY IN June, 1949, and Tim Mara commented: "Steve, you must have struck oil. You had on a new suit yesterday, and you're wearing another new one today."

I had to grin sort of sheepishly and confess: "This isn't a new suit. I have a whole closetful of suits that I wasn't able to wear for five or six years. I grew out of 'em, but it seems as if I've shrunk back into 'em."

My old wardrobe fit me once more because I had shed about sixty pounds in a few months. When my weight climbed over three hundred, the doctor put me on a rigid diet. Everything about me was run down except my weight. I was so played out that I had to take a complete rest in the hospital, and if you don't think football has something to do with it, I do.

The Giants won only two, tied two, and lost eight in 1947. We won four the next year and lost eight, which was some slight improvement, but not enough to save me from thinking of nervous prostration every time I got up on Sunday and realized another game had to be played.

There is nothing more agonizing to a coach than the fact he does not have the men to do a job. The fewer he has, the harder he works. He winds up in the same place as if he had "stood in bed." He gets nowhere, anyway.

We slumped off in 1947–48 immediately after we had won the eastern title in 1946, and the collapse made me feel very sympathetic to many a college coach I had known who had been fired in just such circumstances.

He was a great coach one year, and no coach at all the next season. Or so people said. "Friends" of one year turned out to be shrews the next. School officials who couldn't wait to shake his hand one season became alarmingly and caustically critical of the score each Saturday afternoon. Alumni who met to praise Caesar one season met to bury him the next.

What happened? Was the coach any less the man from one year to another? No, sir. I have known a number of coaches who had to pull up stakes and look for the next job after a losing season, and among them were some of the soundest football men in the country. When they didn't have the horses they couldn't pull the load. Generally, the success or failure of a football team is that simple.

There is nothing more bleak and oppressive than to be part of an outfit which can't reasonably hope to win very often. Tex Coulter, the celebrated tackle of Army's powerful unbeaten teams, summed it up from the player's point of view one day, in regard to our 1947–48 teams on which he played.

"Steve," he said, "I don't ever want to be on a losing team again. We work out all morning, then we study plays all afternoon, and then we come back at night to look at movies and get some more dope. That goes on all week, and when Sunday comes we just take another shellacking. I'll take a winner. With them it's a morning workout, maybe a light session in the afternoon, and we play more football on one Sunday than we could in a season with those bad teams we had."

From a standpoint of manpower, the greatest thrill a

coach can have in the National Football League is to win the bonus pick in the annual draft. I guess you know how that works. The regular draft permits each team to select a man in turn. The draw begins with the team that had the poorest record, and ends with the world champion club.

That is designed to give the weaker teams first chance at the best college players, so that they may, in time, build up to the level of the winning clubs. But that can be unfair to the better clubs, it was decided, because over a period of years these teams might never have a chance to draft one of the half-dozen great name players who come up every season.

Therefore, a bonus pick was adopted, so that each of the twelve entries in the league would be assured first chance once in as many years. At the start of the twelve-year period, a dozen slips are put in a hat, with only one slip marked. Representatives of each team in the league pick a slip, and the one who draws the marked paper is entitled to select his player first, no matter what his position in the regular draft. The next year, only eleven teams pick, and so on, until each of the twelve outfits has had its chance.

Luck of the draw gave me the bonus pick in 1951. Four took slips before me, and I can tell you I was trembling when I put out my hand. That pick can mean so much to a team, and to a coach. It can mean more money at the gate and a higher position in the standings, because the boy selected, in the judgment of football, generally is the No. 1 player of the entire collegiate season.

In 1951 Kyle Rote, of Southern Methodist University was just about the unanimous choice of all clubs, excepting one, which, for geographical reasons, would have selected Leon Heath, of Oklahoma.

Naturally, the Giants took Rote. Poor Kyle didn't have much luck in the 1951 season. He was injured in the exhibitions and suffered a recurrence in the third championship game. We didn't play him thereafter. We figured it would be wiser to rest him up for 1952 and make sure his ailing knee had completely recovered, rather than risk aggravating the injury by letting him work.

Rote underwent an operation in the spring of 1951 at Dallas for removal of damaged cartilage from his knee, and I looked forward to seeing him star in the fall, as I had expected him to do the year before.

Kyle was one player who showed me enough in the brief time he was in uniform to convince me he is a great all-around man. He receives, runs, and kicks with power, polish, and determination. In his first game in Pittsburgh he would have had two touchdowns had he not been green and too eager. Once he ran right over his own blocker, instead of waiting for the latter to clear out an opponent.

In another game he did a beautiful piece of running to go twelve yards for a touchdown. He had to cut, stiff-arm one opponent, and drive through another. He rocketed into the end zone like a real fire horse.

From the first day he reported he did things so naturally and so well and with such rhythm that I had to know he was a great player. But Kyle had a trying time in 1951. He had never been hurt in college, and felt badly about his knee all season.

He worked very hard to get the knee in shape. While we were practicing, Rote would go in the stands and walk up and down the ramps and stairs. For hours we would see him going up and down on left field, right field, and back of home plate.

He was absolutely forlorn when I refused to let him play, and one of my hard jobs that year was convincing him that I had his good at heart and that I did not want to take a chance of having him permanently injured just for the sake of working him a quarter or two. When he realized that, and finally welcomed rest as his only solution, he came out of the dumps and looked to 1952 with keen anticipation. Kyle is a warrior all the way. He was determined to make his mark in big-league football just as he had in college.

I now want to tie two periods together, and explain how teams become good and how teams fail, in our league. I will outline our experiences from 1946, when we did win a title, through the bleak years of 1947–48–49, until we finally came up to the top again in 1950. We didn't win that year. We tied, and were defeated in a play-off by Cleveland, 8–3, but we couldn't have come closer. We were good again, and held our edge through 1951.

Frank Filchock made our attack go in 1946. He was the key in my A formation. He was a hard-hitting runner and a prolific passer, and the combination made him deadly at left half, especially on the optional run-or-pass play. We could not have won without him in 1946. We could not win without him in 1947–48–49, because we did not have a replacement who was backed up with enough competent helpers.

With Filchock gone after '46, and many of our wartime players nearing the end of their string, we had to rebuild. That's not easy, particularly when you start as a winning club, with a late pick in the draft.

We were lucky in 1947 to draw John Cannady, backer-up from Indiana, and Ray Poole, end from Mississippi. We had made a start against the keen competition of the All-America Conference, which was in the second season of its four-year rivalry with the National Football League.

We were able to do much better in '48, mainly because

of a much more favorable position in the draft. We got Charlie Conerly from Mississippi, Joe Scott from San Francisco, Skippy Minisi from Penn, and Bill Swiacki from Columbia, among the nationally known stars.

Now here is a typical case of irony in the football business. We had gone to great pains to get Minisi for our wingback position. He was one of the celebrated players in the country. But somehow he could not make it in our system. Maybe he could in another. He just didn't in ours.

Meanwhile, another boy, whom we did not know existed, walked into our office and asked if we would give him a trial. He was Emlen Tunnell, the first Negro on the Giants, and a boy who was to become one of the spectacular men of the league. That's the way it goes sometimes. At any rate, that's the way it went, and there was no explaining it.

We were able to strengthen our line considerably in 1949 by picking Al DeRogatis, tackle from Duke; Bill Austin, guard from Oregon State; and Jon Baker, guard from California.

Thanks to that manpower, we managed to get back to .500 in 1949, with six won and six lost. We could look more hopefully to the future.

Then things broke our way. The rival All-America Conference disbanded after its fourth year. I'll leave the details to historians. What mattered to me was the news that we were to receive six outstanding players from the Brooklyn–New York squad of the late conference. Mr. Mara told me we were to share top personnel of those AAC Yankees with the New York Bulldogs of the NFL.

At the request of Dan Topping, Stadium president, Buddy Young was excepted. The Negro scatback had been built into a prime gate attraction across the river, and Topping naturally desired to keep him there. Then the

Giants and the Bulldogs picked alternately six times for twelve players on the Brooklyn–New York roster. The remainder went to the Bulldogs, and that name was changed to the Yanks when they moved to the Stadium. After two seasons, the franchise was shifted to Dallas, Texas, leaving the Giants alone in Metropolitan New York City for the first time since 1925.

The former Yankees permitted me to solidify our defense. Among them were Arnie Weinmeister, a great tackle, and the three men who formed the umbrella defense backline with Tunnell—Otto Schnellbacher, Harmon Rowe, and Tom Landry.

We also made advantageous trades to obtain Jim Duncan from Cleveland, Kelly Mote from Detroit, and Bob McChesney from Philadelphia. Duncan proved to be our outstanding defensive end. He played practically every minute on defense in '50 and '51, and did not make a mistake in five games against his original team, the Browns. Mote was immensely valuable because he could play either end, on offense or defense, and was a sure-handed catcher of passes.

There was a story behind our deal for McChesney. Greasy Neale had put Billy Hix, another end, on the waiver list, and the Giants claimed him. Apparently Greasy had wanted Hix all the while, because he offered to swap McChesney for Hix after we claimed the latter. In McChesney we drew an end who, in his second year, was one of the niftiest receivers in the league.

We got additional help in 1950 by drawing three men from the pool of players of the disbanded AAC. We landed Earl Murray, guard from Baltimore; Johnny Rapacz, center from Chicago; and Dick Woodard, center from Los Angeles. Then we had our draft selections, which netted us a rookie backfield of Travis Tidwell, T quarterback from Alabama; Eddie Price, famous fullback from Tulane; and halfbacks Randy Clay, of Texas, and Forrest Griffith, of Kansas.

After long painstaking effort, much costly experimenting with name players who did not always pan out, infinite long-range planning, profitable dealing, and a lot of plain, ordinary luck, we had the team to battle the best. We were able to tie Cleveland for the American Conference title. I might add, in tribute as well as explanation, that Paul Brown had selected and lined up his great team for 1946 and they had played, with only a few changes, for five seasons.

Our job after that was to keep the team going as a unit with new blood. In '51 we added, besides Rote, three first-class ends in Bill Stribling, of Mississippi; Bob Wilkinson, of U.C.L.A.; and Bob Hudson, of Clemson. We also took on a fine all-around back in John Amberg, of Kansas, and several linemen who helped.

When our team wore out in 1946, we were able to replace only about one department a year. There was strong competition in the bidding for personnel, and the job could not be completed for five years. We had to strengthen our line as best we could in '47. We obtained the key man in '48, the great passer Chuck Conerly. The next year we had the chance to complete the line. In '50 we made our defense airtight, added line depth, and began working on the attack, with sound rookie ends and backs. The accent was on the backfield in 1951, with the addition of Rote, and we made our end corps the equal of any in the Conference.

The two flaws in our setup, as developed in the '51 season when we won nine, lost two, and tied one to finish second to Cleveland, were lack of depth in offensive guards, and no reserves in halfbacks, because of Rote's injury.

As a result, for 1952 we could concentrate our early draft picks on those positions. As No. 1 we selected Frank Gifford, the brilliant all-around All-America halfback of U.S.C., and as No. 2 Ray Beck, who caught the eye of the All-America selectors as a guard for Georgia Tech.

We also added two backs who were among the nation's leaders, the somewhat fabulous Fred Benners, of S.M.U., and raceaway outside runner Frank Smith, of Miami U. We had selected these men a year before they completed school. The NFL permits drafting of players in the year their original class graduates, no matter how long they may remain in school thereafter or what their college football eligibility might be.

Naturally, we must wait until amateurs have finished their college sports careers before signing them, but picking outstanding men a year before they are available is like putting money in the bank. And only the rich can afford it—that is, only a club so well-fixed for the upcoming season that it can spare a draft pick on a man for the following season. When we became "rich" in 1950, we were in position to gamble on "futures." Benners and Smith were two dividends of that policy. Had we not picked these two boys in advance, we would have stood hardly any chance to draw either in the year they graduated.

This is an effort to show how difficult it is to build a title contender. When you have one, you must be on the alert to make sure it doesn't go to ruin on you. It's essential to bring in good new material each season to replace older veterans who have lost a step of their speed. You have to plan two or three years ahead to avoid a vital weakness at any one position. Generally, a team is in danger of going over the hill as a championship force when its average age goes much higher than twenty-five years. It is wise to hold close to that figure, or below it if possible, if quality reinforcements are available. Naturally, you won't always succeed; unexpected circumstances will upset your well-laid plans.

On the average, though, a rookie will not be a winning factor for most of his opening year. He slowly learns the tricks of the pro trade. One fellow who did prove a natural was Ward Cuff. He had amazing confidence in himself. He was a regular from the start.

Ward had a storybook beginning as a pro. Before his first game at Pittsburgh, in which he was to work at defensive right half, I cautioned him: "Cuff, the other fellows know you're a rookie. When they see you in there they'll surely try to throw a pass over your head. How about it? Are you going to be faked right out of the game?"

"Coach," he replied, "if they throw a pass like that, I'll pick it off sure for a touchdown!"

He did exactly that. On Pittsburgh's second play they tried to beat Cuff, and he intercepted for a sixty-yard touchdown. Ward was a regular from that moment.

Most rookies, however, sit it out a while. Even so talented a passer as Ed Danowski kept us company on the bench for his first month as a rookie. Ed had a lot of relatives and friends out at Riverhead, Long Island, and he would get tickets for them every week. They were like a hired claque. They would chant all day long, "We want Danowski, we want Danowski—"

About the third game, I turned to Ed in the second quarter and yelled: "Danowski—on your feet." Ed stripped off his jacket and came running over, ready and eager to annihilate the opposition.

"Ed," I said, "some of your friends are yelling for you up in the stands. Go see what they want."

Danowski became a successful coach at his alma mater, Fordham, and has often told that one on himself.

Danowski was one of those exceptional players who were able to stay in championship competition over a long period. He was on our championship team in 1934 and was still in action when we won in 1941. That's always proof of professional football greatness.

The average is not so high in years. Some players can hold their jobs only a few seasons on a top-flight team. Others, built for the long haul, can go six, seven, eight. The truly outstanding person, of unsurpassed talent and durability can go as long as fifteen years. Mel Hein and Sam Baugh are two who defied the years. But it is rare to find a ten-year man among the pros. The average, with good teams in the running, probably isn't as high as five, and is more than likely around four.

I can show that is true. The Giants had two title eras before the war, when the best college boys were available. The game was on a stable basis, so far as personnel went, before the long drought of wartime set in. We won for three years, 1933–34–35, and then again over two years, in 1938–39.

Only seven men of the '33–'34–'35 teams were able to extend their careers into '38–'39. They were Dale Burnett, Johnny Dell Isola, Kink Richards, Leland Shaffer, Ken Strong, Danowski, and Hein. Strong, one of the all-time great backs, from N.Y.U., was with us in '33, and also on hand, as a kicker, in '46, when we won. Hein's career with championship clubs went from '33 through '44. Danowski and Shaffer, the latter one of the superior blocking backs, both played from the '33–'34–'35 era into our title year of '41.

Even from '39 to '41 we had a turnover of considerable size. Only fifteen men of the '39 champions were on hand in '41, on a squad numbering thirty-three. They were Tuffy Leemans, Kayo Lunday, Johnny Mellus, Doug Oldershaw, Jim Poole, Hank Soar, Will Walls, Frank Cope, Nello Falaschi, Jim Lee Howell, Shaffer, Strong, Danowski, Hein, and Cuff.

Even in the '33 to '35 period, of three years, there were only eleven men of the '33 team holding over through '35. They were Red Badgro, Dale Burnett, Stu Clancy, Len Grant, Tex Irvin, Tom Jones, Bo Molenda, Bill Morgan, Kink Richards, Strong, and Hein.

You can easily see that, with such a turnover in manpower, a coach had better make sure his rookies are good, or he will soon be without a sound team. He will have a bunch of fellows with reputations, but without their former speed. Then he loses his speed too, and the walk from the clubhouse to the field becomes longer and longer every week.

Sometimes, when a club approaches the danger mark in average age, it is much better to go all the way with rookies, if enough of quality are procurable. We did that in 1937, the year we introduced the A formation, with as fine a group of young players as we ever did have. Those kids lost three games in '37, two in '38, and one in '39. Outstanding rookies in the lot were Chuck Gelatka, of Mississippi State; Orville Tuttle, of Oklahoma City U.; Ox Parry, of Baylor; Ed Widseth, of Minnesota; Tarzan White, of Alabama; Cuff, of Marquette; Soar, of Providence; Jim Poole, of Mississippi; Walls, of T.C.U.; and Jim Lee Howell and Lunday, of Arkansas.

Again in '41 we went with youth, when we lined up a gang of outstanding boys. Among them were Vince Dennery and Len Eshmont, of Fordham; Frank Reagan, of

Penn; Chuck Gladchuk, of Boston College; George Franck, of Minnesota; Jack Lummus, of Baylor; Marion Pugh, of Texas A. & M.; Len Younce, of Oregon State; and Andy Marefos, of St. Mary's in California. Most of those boys went into military service after winning in '41.

As you might suspect, it isn't easy to build a championship team. It is sometimes even more difficult to get the one player who will act as leader of the group. Without this leader, even a high-quality squad may not attain its potential consistency. It may not even jell. I mean a boy such as Arnie Weinmeister, our great tackle, who has the personality and the integrity of judgment which induce the other fellows to look up to him. He acts as an inspiration, too, with his tireless, outstanding play in which his terrific and sustained speed often enables him to handle his position and still help out other boys who may be a little weak in certain angles.

On attack, a leader is an essential. Naturally, he will be the signal-caller. If he is the man who handles the ball, the quarterback in the T, or the left halfback in the single wing, all the better.

One of the first requisites in such a man is the ability to evaluate his teammates, so that he will call the right man for the right assignment and never demand a job that is beyond a man's capability. You will often strike on a fellow for your signal-caller only to find that, while he has excellent judgment outside the ten-yard line, he has none at all inside the ten. Other boys may be just the opposite. The trick is to find the all-around fellow, who can appraise his chances correctly wherever he stands.

Your leader must have the quick mind to size up the defense against him after two series of downs, at most. If he is in doubt, he should take time out to quiz his linemen and ends. That used to be an easy job when I played and defense men stayed put in the seven-man line setups.

Nowadays it is a difficult job, what with shifting defenses of all kinds. The quarterback has to figure, from his observation, how he can vary his blocking to exert necessary pressure no matter how the defense deploys. He has to figure out the schemes which will take advantage of repeated mistakes by an opposing player, because that is the easy way to touchdowns.

The quarterback should rally his team by being the first man in the huddle. He should call plays with snap and authority. If he drags, his team will drag. He sets the tempo. It's the same in coaching. If a coach has no fire or if he is deadpan, the team reflects it. He may have a bunch of good workers, but in time his negative personality will get them down and have them acting his way. The attitude or feeling of a coach or quarterback is contagious and very quickly transferred to an entire squad.

A quarterback must keep his team under control at all times, and he must not allow carping or criticism. If a boy makes an error, that boy knows it before anybody, and as well as anybody. If the quarterback shows resentment, he is not a leader. The smart leader will pat that poor kid on the back and restore his confidence.

A great example was Tuffy Leemans. I've seen Tuffy make many a run when the blocking was not up to standard. But upon returning to the huddle to call the next signal, the first thing he'd say was: "Nice blocking, gang. Let's hit 'em again." He always gave his mates credit. If a man didn't do his best, he simply had to have a self-indicting feeling of guilt when he heard Tuffy's compliments. Pride forced him to go out and do better. That is simple psychology, but it wasn't studied in Leemans. It was natural and unforced, a subtle and constructive thing.

The great quarterbacks allow no interference from any

other player, but they can insist on that in a nice way without antagonizing a fellow. There is a type of player who, in a mistaken idea he is being helpful, rushes into the huddle with a request to run this or that play. He has only partial knowledge, while the quarterback is charged with knowing as much of the whole picture as he can. Those players can only confuse the signal-caller. On our club no player may talk to the quarterback unless asked a question, or until time is out. Then he may bring up any subject.

We have a method of dealing with volunteer quarter-backs. We try to discover 'em in training camp, and that is never a difficult job. Nor does it take long. Once identi-fied, the self-nominated leader is allowed to go in and call plays. He soon finds out he can't do it. He's cured. But if, by chance, he can do it, we really try to make a quarterback out of him. But I have known many who thought they were and weren't, and never one who could do it without our having a good idea he could beforehand. It's our job to see these things ahead of time. It would be a good idea to get some of our noisiest grandstand quarter-backs to walk behind the team and call the plays and see how far they would advance the ball. Unfortunately, I've never been able to do that. The grandstand coaches never let us in on their strategy until after the game. Maybe if they got it in before, it might work. Then again, it might not.

There are two factors in quarterbacking which the av-erage fan cannot appreciate. One is the very brief time the signal-caller has at his command, after carrying out his own assignment, to make what often can be a vital decision. He can't think it over. First, he may have a better idea an instant after the ball is snapped. He often does. But then it's too late. The other factor is the great number of plays which a fan may believe to be wrong calls, but which are sound calls. They fail of fruition because of a trifling error not observed in the stands.

Studying the movies, as we do, discloses play after play which is missed by the narrowest of margins. A defensive man may slide off a block just far enough to get a hold on the ball-carrier, or even push him off stride. A carrier can be tripped, purely by accident, when he has blocking set up for a pretty play. There can be a momentary juggling of the ball as it is handed off by the quarterback, and that will ruin the play. There are so many little details which can go wrong through no fault in the quarterback's call, that I could go on for hours relating case after case. Important, however, is that we study each other's mistakes and look each other in the eye, not with contempt, but with thorough understanding of failings.

I believe in giving the quarterback full responsibility in selection of plays. I believe he is in the best position, if he has the football acumen, to call the play most apt to gain.

Some coaches like to send in plays in varying degrees. Some like to have complete command from the bench, so that their quarterback is always under orders. Others will intrude only at what they deem to be key points.

I will go all the way with my signal-caller if he can satisfy me he has the temperament and the competence in judgment to do a good job for me. You cannot build responsibility in a young fellow by denying him the right to exercise it. That goes for everything—football and life itself.

I believe a boy will do a better job when he has the responsibility on his shoulders. I believe he will play better and induce a higher morale in his group. Certainly the rest of the team will have more respect for him, and be more inclined to put out for him, when they know he carries all that weight.

I can call plays from the bench all day long, but I know, from my experience as a player, that a certain percentage will be sent in at moments when my team knows something else will do better. Denying even occasionally the value of their observation and judgment is bound to lower their assurance, because that puts them in the position of running a play without faith in its success. That weakens individual confidence, and it doesn't take long to spread through the squad.

I am going to help my quarterback all I can from the bench, when he wants advice. But I do not believe in overruling him or making him a robot out there, if I can help it.

Every quarterback is close to his coach to begin with. First of all, he has absorbed the coach's thinking on general strategy. He has gone over scouting reports with the coach for each particular foe and has discussed the plays which have the best chance, in prospect, for every game.

Then, in the game, he has the benefit of information relayed to him from the phone man, who is valuable in spotting unsound deployment of defense. The coach will offer information from his observation, too.

Everybody helps the quarterback; none should interfere with him.

No coach could have instructed Arnie Herber, a great passer of Green Bay history, when he threw three touchdowns in six minutes as a Giant in 1944. Arnie spotted the left halfback of the Eagles making a break forward on a particular play to defend against a rush. He tried it again and got the same reaction. That halfback was charging to within five yards of the line. Herber switched to a variation to get Frank Liebel, end, behind that half-back. It worked for a touchdown. Then Herber played that boy like a piano. When the halfback retreated so that he was too deep, about fifteen yards back, Arnie crossed Liebel in front of him and scored another touchdown. The confused kid went back to his original charge, and Liebel caught another on him.

Passing is something no coach can execute for his quarterback. The coach is absolutely in the hands of the man who is throwing. If he is a chap who can become conscious of rushers when the going gets hot, then he is going to lose sight of his downfield receivers and any call he makes is likely to be a poor one. On the other hand, there are many crack passers who will stand up to heavy traffic, make a brilliant play, and then receive no credit at all from the average fan.

For instance, on a shoestring catch, the receiver generally is the fellow who draws the praise. But that shoe-string play is planned very often when a team is close to the goal. It is thrown, and with marvelous accuracy, to the only spot that the defense cannot guard adequately. Mac Speedie is very good at shoestring catches, and Otto Graham shoots them to him well. But you will only hear Graham lauded for those longies he throws out in the open with a touchdown threat.

When a coach finally assembles a good team and then gets a quarterback who can fake, throw, run, think, and command the respect of the squad, he is a lucky fellow who can sit down and relax for a brief spell—before he begins worrying about next week.

10

~~~~~~~~~~~~~~~

THE GIANTS TRAINED IN SUPERIOR, WISCONSIN, IN 1949, AND Bronko Nagurski, who lived at International Falls, Minnesota, about a hundred and fifty miles away, drove over to see me one day. Bronko was the truly fabulous fullback of the Chicago Bears who was at his peak in the early thirties. I had played against him, and we had come to respect each other after meeting head on from time to time through the years. I never claimed I could stop Nagurski, any more than I ever insisted I could walk through a steel door, but I believe I did as well as any other tackle to annoy the Bronko. Tacklers to Nagurski were like the flies on the flanks of a horse—a nuisance but not serious.

Bronko had brought along his son, a happy-looking redhead of ten, who didn't have the size as yet but showed the makings of his old man. Nagurski spent most of the day with us, and he surely impressed our boys when he came into the mess hall for lunch. There was still the air about him, a disarming smile, the firm neck, and the trim look to his body, that suggested he could tear the place apart if he had a mind to, but mightn't if folks were careful not to rile him.

When the Nagurskis left we all went out on the porch to say good-by. As Bronko opened the door of his car, he turned to us, and the boy did too, but the little fellow kept backing up, and got a smart whack alongside the head from the door of the car.

Someone near me exclaimed: "Wow! That kid will have a good cry!"

I snapped back: "Not Nagurski's boy!"

I don't know why I came out with that, but it certainly was an instinctive indication of the admiration I held for Nagurski. His boy didn't cry, either.

The Bronko was so rugged as a player that I ordered the Giants to simply avoid tackling him head on, in the championship play-off of 1933, which the Bears won 23–21. What I did was assign two men to cover him, and three on certain plays. They were to throw themselves in front of him, blockwise, in hopes of tripping him or knocking him off stride, so that the rest could fall on him like a wolf pack. The Bronko still gained even when two or three tacklers got a hold.

In that way I did sacrifice a few yards now and then, but I made sure he didn't break loose. What was more important, I didn't lose men trying to butt the Bronko down. You may remember the story of my first five-man line, which Nagurski ruined by knocking Hank Reese, our middle backer-up, out cold. Reese wasn't much use the rest of the season. He tells me even today that he can still hear a strange buzzing in his head now and then, and I wouldn't bet he's kidding.

Nagurski was the only back I have ever seen who ran his own interference. He has to be my all-time big-league fullback.

I take him over Ernie Nevers, who came before him, and whom we have already met in this story, and over Clark Hinkle, of the Green Bay Packers, who followed him as the league's finest. Hinkle was exceptional over a spectacular period of ten years. He could do just about everything. He was a place-kicker and punter. He could play defense, and he had a lot of heart. He could jar you in the old-fashioned way, or run wide, and he maintained hitting ability when he used his outside speed. Every time he played the Giants he seemed to have hard luck and leave with injuries. No matter how battered up he might be, Hinkle would have himself strapped together with a bandage here and a bandage there and always get back in action for the final quarter.

But Nagurski hit the hardest. He was the one and only.

Although I know and have stated that the teams of my playing days could not compare with those of today, I do not mean that to apply to the truly great players of old times. The early teams lacked the all-over speed and depth to match the average outfit of today, but the individual stars would be commanding in any era. That they played a different game, both in strategic conception and in working tactics, doesn't matter. They had the qualities, and proved them, to be outstanding in any kind of football, as I will show in discussing my all-time team.

First, let's put down their names. It is generally difficult to pick and choose among such a tremendous total of celebrated names as we have had in big-league football, both All-America stickouts of college and those who came obscurely into the pros to make their reputation.

But I have no doubt these eleven are my best. I have thought them over through the years, and have been quizzed on the subject hundreds of times. I always hold firm for these eleven:

Ends: Guy Chamberlain and Don Hutson.
Tackles: Cal Hubbard and Link Lyman.
Guards: Mike Michalske and Danny Fortmann.

Center: Mel Hein.
Quarterback: Sammy Baugh.
Halfbacks: Red Grange and Steve Van Buren.
Fullback: Bronko Nagurski.

Chamberlain starred at Nebraska and then played professionally with Canton, Cleveland, and the Frankford Yellow Jackets of the twenties. Hutson, from Alabama, was Green Bay's greatest in the late thirties and early forties.

Hubbard, from Geneva College, was with the Giants and the Packers in the late twenties and early thirties. Lyman, from Nebraska, was a Bears star in the twenties.

Michalske worked for Green Bay in the mid-thirties after leaving Penn State, and Fortmann, a Colgate alumnus, was a Bear in the late thirties and early forties. Hein played fifteen years for New York, beginning in 1931.

Baugh, from Texas Christian U., and the greatest passer out of the Southwest, first played for the Redskins in 1937 and was still on deck for 1952. Grange, who did so much to focus public interest on football, both as a collegian and as a professional, starred with the Bears and the New York Yankees in the twenties and early thirties after graduating from Illinois.

Van Buren, from L.S.U., still a member of the Philadelphia Eagles, carried that team to the world championship while he captured practically all the rushing records in the book. Nagurski came from Minnesota to the Bears.

Examine that team, and you will find that every man "knew the score." Each one was above average in awareness of the changing situations of a game, and each had the ability, far above average, to make something of his knowledge.

Another point I want to stress. Every one of these fellows is a sixty-minute man, if need be. These men are not a platoon—they form a team. Every one has proved himself to be excellent on defense as well as offense, except Van Buren, whom I would rate good but not superlative. But Van Buren, as he became more valuable as a ball-carrier, gradually was withheld from defense, when he was improving in that phase of the game.

Also, every man has proved his high quality over a long period. Durability has to be a test of an all-time player.

Chamberlain was the shrewdest opportunist I have ever seen. He was uncanny in "smelling out" a play or a mistake. His shrewdness could beat the other team in every way which is possible. He was the fellow who invariably came up with the fumble, the blocked kick, the interception, as well as the pass thrown by his own man, which would win a game.

Hutson was the greatest receiver who ever lived. He could fake both of two good men assigned to cover him, and he had the speed to turn any opening into a touchdown. In the record books, his is the name you read time and again. Now and then a player will break one of his records, but seldom two. And Hutson set them all. In setting them, he made a few passers famous. Don was also a crack defense man, at safety or left half.

Hubbard, at 260, and Lyman, at 250, would form a classic tackles team. My own pair of Arnie Weinmeister and Al DeRogatis remind me of them. Cal, with his combination of speed, weight, and timing, was a devastating blocker. He could play end, and did. On defense he made them run the other way. Lyman was the ingenious tackle whom I have already cited for his discovery of splits in line play.

Fortmann, at 185–190, and Michalske, at 215–220, were the sprinter-type guards who could pull out of line to throw a block anywhere in their team's striking area. Michalske was one of the first to give away a little weight for speed, as the game changed from the brute-force era. Fortmann, although on the light side, was unexcelled at diagnosing a play. He was always "looking at you," almost impossible to trap, and nifty when he threw a block.

Hein was just a natural football player who came up ready-made, able to do everything. Teaching him was like teaching Babe Ruth to hit. At 225–230, Mel was a dynamic offensive blocker, a most accurate snapper, and a genius at backing up the line. Hein could discourage the most accomplished attacking stars who ever lived.

Baugh's matchless passing may hide other qualities which made him truly the all-around ball player. He was a terror at quick-kicking from his original single-wing formation, and he used that kick as a dangerous pressure weapon. He was a runner, and gained over two hundred yards his first season, until he was restrained from carrying the ball because of fear of injury to his great arm. He was, for some years, as astute a safety man as you would want, and in 1943 set a league record for interceptions—since surpassed—of eleven in ten games.

Baugh's peculiar value as a passer was his ability to stand alone as the game-winner, with any ends and not one of all-star caliber. I always thought Hein, a great diagnostician, summed that up best, during a 1944 interview in which he was asked to compare Sid Luckman, of the Bears, Cecil Isbell, of the Packers, and Baugh. I have that clipping, because it expressed exactly my thoughts on Baugh.

"In brief," Hein was quoted, "Baugh is the best, and the best I have ever seen. Baugh's strongest-throwing and most accurate arm would give any club that had him a chance to be great. He is as close as anyone can come to being a one-man team, because he can win by himself. Luckman and Isbell, while also unquestionably great passers, do not dominate the game like Baugh, because team considerations enter their cases. For Isbell, it is Don Hutson's pass-catching ability—he and not Isbell was the league's most valuable player last year. For Luckman, it is the Bears' running game which sets up his passes. With any other club, either Isbell or Luckman might not be so outstanding. But with Baugh, all he needs is someone to hang onto the ball—he'll hit the man in any circumstances."

Baugh, of course, has had excellent receivers, but he also has made a long succession of ends and halfbacks look good through the years. Sam says Dick Todd, halfback, and more recently coach of the Redskins, was his favorite receiver. I thought Wayne Millner was his most dangerous receiver. In the 1937 play-off, a Washington win by 28–21, Millner performed an outstanding job on a frozen field by making two long runs after receiving passes, for both touchdowns.

It is always difficult to apportion the credit when you have an established hookup of a star passer and a star receiver making most of your aerial touchdowns. It is hard to make it better than 50-50 between the two men in such superlative combinations as Dunn and Dillweg, Isbell and Hutson, Herber and Blood of the Packers, Luckman and Kavanaugh of the Bears, Thompson and Ferrante of the Eagles, Albert and Soltau of the Forty-Niners, Layne and Hart of the Lions, Christman and Dewell of the Cardinals, Waterfield and Fears, and Van Brocklin and Hirsch of the Rams, Graham and Speedie, and Graham and Lavelli of the Browns, Danowski and Burnett, Danowski and Flaherty, and Conerly and Swiacki of the Giants.

But Baugh has made all his receivers look good, and he has taken them as they come.

Grange, the Galloping Ghost of Illinois, had so much richly deserved publicity over his running that the public probably was not aware of his sterling value as an all-around player. He was one of the best blockers I ever faced, and he was simply terrific as a defensive back. At 180–185 pounds Red had everything as a runner, speed, shiftiness, and power.

Van Buren can go all the way on any play. He has to be stopped before he gets up a head of steam, behind the line or at it, unless the defense wants to risk a touchdown. Steve combines speed, weight, and drive, at 205 pounds. When he is hit in the line, he can lower his head and drive for the first down. In the open he is too much for any one man, because he has the speed to run around most, and the power to drive through any. He is the surpassing runner in the record books as well as on the field. He takes a place in that regard with Baugh at passing and Hutson at receiving.

I don't have to stress the offensive qualities of my all-time team. On defense, it would be equally outstanding. With that personnel I could work with a virtual four-man line if I wanted, as I did with the Giants in 1950 and 1951, because tackles Lyman and Hubbard would anchor a line as Weinmeister and DeRogatis did for the Giants, to give the ends almost complete freedom to reddog or drift or drop. As for backers-up, I would have only the best in Hein and Nagurski. No one could ask finer middle men than Michalske and Fortmann.

With Grange and Van Buren at halfback and Baugh at safety, I would probably use a basic 6-2-3, which, of course, would be adaptable to almost any variation because of the liberties my ends could take, the stanchness of the line with Lyman and Hubbard, and the strength of the backers-up, with either Hein or Nagurski able to hold that position without the other, if one should be more valuable moved up or dropped back.

I'll never see that team together, and, while I would like to, I'm sure no rival in the league would want to.

Among the Giant teams I have played on or coached, I must regard our champions of 1938 as the finest group. This club won eight, lost two, and tied one, and defeated the Green Bay Packers for the world title. The '38 squad was easily the high-scoring outfit in the eastern division, and had a remarkable defensive record, unapproached in the league, of only seventy-nine points allowed in eleven games—about one touchdown a game. This outfit had the greatest spirit and team co-ordination of any championship club I have ever been connected with.

It was a young team, with nine rookies and twelve second-year men. The personnel was as follows:

Ends: Ray Hanken, of George Washington; Jim Lee Howell, of Arkansas; Jim Poole, of Mississippi; Will Walls, of T.C.U.; Jiggs Kline, of Emporia; and Chuck Gelatka, of Mississippi State.

Tackles: John Mellus, of Villanova; Frank Cope, of Santa Clara; Ed Widseth, of Minnesota; Pete Cole, of Trinity (Texas); and Jack Haden, of Arkansas.

Guards: John Dell Isola, of Fordham; Tarzan White, of Alabama; Kayo Lunday, of Arkansas; Orville Tuttle, of Oklahoma City; and Ox Parry, of Baylor.

Centers: Mel Hein, of Washington State; Larry Johnson, of Haskell; and Stan Galazin, of Villanova.

Backs: Ed Danowski, of Fordham; Nello Falaschi, of Santa Clara; Tuffy Leemans, of George Washington; Len Barnum, of West Virginia Wesleyan; Kink Richards, of Simpson (Iowa) College; Ward Cuff, of Marquette; Hank

Soar, of Providence; Hugh Wolfe, of Texas; Dale Burnett, of Emporia; Leland Shaffer, of Kansas State; and John Gildea, of St. Bonaventure.

I rate that crew over my own 1927 herd of champion bone-twisters, and over our 1934 world champions starring Ken Strong and with what I believe to have been the greatest pair of all-around ends the game has known— Morris Badgro and Ray Flaherty. Those two were a team of redheaded destroyers, second to none.

When I am asked to select an all-time Giants team, as I have been so often, I make two reservations. I do not select any player on the club at the time I make the pick, and I will not limit myself to eleven men, but prefer to name a squad.

I name twenty-three men. This squad is not an offensive team, nor a defensive platoon. It is both. Every player is a sixty-minute man. Any eleven of them could play a game without help. Here they are, from all parts of the country:

Ends: Jim Poole, of Mississippi; Ray Flaherty, of Gonzaga; and Morris Badgro, of U.S.C.

Tackles: Al Blozis, of Georgetown; Ed Widseth, of Minnesota; and Cal Hubbard, of Geneva.

Guards: Len Younce, of Oregon State; John Dell Isola, of Fordham; and Butch Gibson, of Grove City (Pa.) College.

Centers: Mel Hein, of Washington State; George Murtaugh, of Georgetown; and Joe Alexander, of Syracuse.

Quarterbacks: Ed Danowski, of Fordham; Bennie Friedman, of Michigan; Cecil Griggs, of Sherman (Texas) College; and Jack Hagerty, of Georgetown.

Halfbacks: Tuffy Leemans, of George Washington; Kink Richards, of Simpson (Iowa) College; Ward Cuff, of Marquette; and Hinkey Haines, of Penn State.

Fullbacks: Ken Strong, of N.Y.U.; Jack McBride, of Syracuse; and Phil White, of Oklahoma.

These men appeared on divisional championship teams as follows: Hagerty, Hubbard, White, and Murtaugh in '27; McBride in '27–'33; Flaherty and Gibson in '33–'34; Badgro in '33–'34–'35; Richards in '33–'34–'35–'38–'39; Strong in '33–'34–'35–'39–'44–'46; Dell Isola, in '34–'35–'38–'39; Danowski in '34–'35–'38–'39–'41; Widseth in '38–'39; Leemans in '38–'39–'41; Cuff in '38–'39–'41–'44; Poole in '38–'39–'41–'46; and Younce in '41–'44–'46.

Friedman, Griggs, Blozis, and Alexander did not play for championship squads. Friedman worked between our '27 and '33 winners. Griggs was with the original Giants of 1925 and retired before we lined up for '27. Blozis, a rookie of 1942, was killed with our armed forces in Europe in 1945. Alexander was an original Giant who withdrew from football to study medicine.

The squad I have selected is tuned to the T, our basic formation nowadays, and the four men at quarterback were single-wing halfbacks in reality. But all would have been surpassingly good T-men.

I would like to single out several more players for special skills. Nello Falaschi, of Santa Clara, and Leland Shaffer, of Kansas State, were truly great blockers at the quarterback spot in my A formation.

Dale Burnett, of Emporia, was my most effective pass receiver, Kay Eakin, of Arkansas, the most brilliant punter, Hein the peerless tackler, Cuff the finest field-goal kicker, Strong the star at kickoffs, and Danowski the most skillful passer.

The ends on my all-time Giants team were flawless on offense and defense. Poole was big and rugged and implacable. Flaherty was a terrific receiver and a good punter. He and Badgro, die-hard redheads who couldn't stand losing, were blasting blockers offensively.

I believe Blozis would have been the greatest tackle in history, if he could have been spared to us. He was an absolute wave of terror when he made his move, and could wipe out two, three, four men at times with his speed, power, and reach, on offense or defense. I regard Widseth as my top offensive lineman, although he was twenty-seven before he came up from Minnesota. Hubbard, as good an end and line backer as he was a tackle, was one of the naturals of football.

Dell Isola combined intense desire to play with boundless talent and was a superb line backer and pass defender as well as a smart offensive guard. Younce was a remarkable punter, and a crack blocker pulling out of line. He was a leader who called our defense signals and could back up the line. Gibson, a real tough cookie, was one of the first of the running guards, and had the speed to outrun many backs of his time.

Hein played longer than any Giant and was coached less. Murtaugh had such speed as a center that he often filled in at end with distinction. Alexander, one of the all-time heroes of Syracuse, was the only man I ever saw play with one shoulder pad. He always tackled and blocked with his right shoulder, and didn't see the need of toting extra, unnecessary weight. The one pad he wore was skinned down, at that.

Danowski never passed at Fordham, but he indicated he was a natural as a thrower when he came to the Giants. We had quite a time convincing him he could do the job. I remember one game when Ed complained that his shoulder hurt and said that Leemans ought to throw. I insisted Danowski make a try. He completed ten out of eleven in the first half, four for touchdowns. At half time

I told him: "Too bad your arm bothers you, Ed. You better not throw any more today."

Danowski never paid any attention to a rusher. He never took his eyes off his receivers. He threw many a pass which he never saw completed, when he rifled the ball as he was hit and went down. He had great receivers in Burnett, Flaherty, Badgro, and Leemans, and our running game was always sound enough to lend surprise to his passes. Ed holds the record for fewest passes intercepted over a long period, and it is an amazing record. Over seven years, only forty-two of his passes were stolen by the defense— six a season.

Friedman was one of the passers who made the new air weapon important in football. He threw an easy ball to handle, and was extraordinarily accurate at long range.

Griggs came to us from Canton, where he handled such smart Indians as Thorpe, Guyon, and Kalac. Griggs could do anything, and as an analyst he was unsurpassed. After he ran three plays he could take time out and brief us on the moves of every defensive player. He had camera eyes.

Hagerty, an outstanding passer and runner, was the greatest safety man I have seen. In five years, I never saw him fumble or drop a punt, or lose a pass he got his hands on.

Leemans was one of the ranking players of the league. He had the respect of his opponents as well as the Giants. He was not fast, but his change of pace was uncanny, and he always seemed to be running with a touchdown in prospect. Fans remember him as a runner, but he was a deadly clutch passer, as the defense guarded him for a rush. In '38 and '39, we often alternated him with Danowski at the left half passing spot.

Leemans is best remembered for his hips. Tacklers would bounce off those hips. He would roll and pivot with a tackler, shake him loose, and come up running. I have seen him go down four or five times on a touchdown run, and it was hard to be sure he had ever broken his stride. It seemed as though he could run when he was flat on the ground.

Leeman's secret was this: if he was within three yards of a tackler, Tuffy figured he had that man beat and would look for the next one eight to ten yards downfield. The average back concentrates on the nearest threat, and a subsequent one therefore comes as a surprise to him. Tuffy figured out his future while he was making a touchdown tour.

Leemans was not a big name as a college player at George Washington U., but was among seventy boys selected for the All-Star squad to play the NFL champions in Chicago. One day in scrimmage a halfback was hurt, and Bernie Bierman, coach of the All-Stars, yelled for a halfback. Tuffy was fastest off the bench and got the job. In that scrimmage he ran for four touchdowns, with the longest a dash of seventy yards. He made the first team right there, and played well against the professionals.

When he came into New York the following month, as a member of the Eastern All-Stars who opposed the Giants, we were scared to death of his running ability but didn't want to risk hurting him, because he became a Giant the day after that game.

Leemans, in the first quarter, ran a punt back sixty-five yards against us. One of our fellows got up from the bench and began screaming to our gang on the field: "Hit him, but don't hurt him!"

After we had Leemans with us for a while we discovered it was hard to hit him and almost impossible to hurt him.

Richards came unheralded from a small school, Simpson College, to break the game wide open with his dazzling running. He was cute. He had speed. He could cut. He could shake tacklers. He was big enough to drive, too.

Cuff was one of the great place-kickers who never did kick in college. The first time we used him as a place-kicker he booted field goals for forty-two and forty-three yards to win the game 6–0. Ward was outstanding as a runner, a receiver, and a defensive halfback. Above all, he was an Iron Man who could play with so many injuries that he often seemed to be taped from head to toe before he put on his uniform.

Haines specialized in speed running and was dangerous on passes and punts as well as from scrimmage. McBride was a good place-kicker and a durable runner with exceptional starting speed which would have made him even more outstanding in the T. White was a block buster when he hit the line, had passing skill, and amazing control in placing punts. Strong was just great. He was a blocker, kicker, runner on the highest level.

He had speed, and he also could bowl fellows out of his way. He was a league star over a long period, from 1933 through 1947, and is the leading scorer of the Giants, with 351 points in the eight years he played for us.

It is pleasant to look to the past, to revive the spectacular feats of the great players. A coach can't get hurt looking backward. However, as a coach, I have felt eager to peer ahead, without a shudder of alarm, since we began pushing away up from .500 in 1949. But a coach is optimistic only at his own peril, and I will get off the air right now, before I talk too much.

11

A MAN IS LUCKY WHO HAS A JOB THAT DOESN'T SEEM LIKE work to him. I've been lucky that way because I have enjoyed football from the time I started, and still regard it as a game. I remember the first professional game I ever played, as a real pro in the National League. It was in Milwaukee and was so much different from the college ball I'd been used to in the Southwest, and had so much smarter and more talented boys, that I was sold on it right there. I didn't see how people who liked sports could help liking the big-league variety of football.

When the Mara family a few years back presented me with a sterling silver service in honor of my twenty-fifth year with the Giants, I could honestly feel that I should have been giving them the presents, along with my thanks for a wonderful time. I said that the twenty-five years had been like a vacation to me, and that's exactly what I meant.

I am very grateful to football for what it has done for me. I think any number of athletes will tell you the same thing. My associations . . . the fine people I've dealt with . . . the thrills every Sunday . . . the grand young boys I meet and teach . . . they add up to as good a deal as ever could happen to anybody.

The Maras could not have been kinder to me. I never

had a contract from the time I got the job, and there has never been a mention of one. Yet I have heard of coaches who held term contracts and still failed to last a single season. Seasons, for instance, such as I had in '47 and '48, when we won only six games in two years and when I imagine more than a few fans were yelling for my thinning scalp.

My dealings with my bosses have always been direct, friendly, and practical, not only with Mr. Mara, but with his two boys, Jack, who is the president, and Wellington, who is secretary-treasurer. In fact, Wellington practically grew up in camp with the football teams. The first time he ever stayed away from home overnight, I had him in camp at Pearl River, New York. Mrs. Mara was worried about him, and warned me not to let him get hurt. The second day there, Mel Hein ran over him and blacked his eye. Our press agent at that time had a strange slant on publicity and let Mrs. Mara know about it. She wanted her boy home, but I managed to talk her out of that, and Wellington has been a regular ever since, except for his hitch in the Navy.

I guess Mrs. Mara doesn't worry any more; Jack somehow got tangled in a play a few years back at Saranac Lake, New York, and I didn't hear from headquarters about that one.

There is no thrill to me like getting up on a Sunday morning, looking at breakfast for half an hour and leaving it there, walking out the right door so as not to hex the day, and then going out to the park, full of butterflies just as it was over twenty-five years ago, wondering whether the scheming and the thinking is going to turn out all right.

I have had many great games with the Giants as player and coach, but I have to make my top thrill the 1934 play-off with the Bears in the Polo Grounds. The Bears were unbeaten, while we had managed to squeak through an awful dogfight in the eastern division with an eight-won, five-lost record, and the Chicago "monsters of the midway," as they were called by some of the press, were huge favorites. They seemed entitled to the role as they led us 13–3 at half time.

Then the fun began. It was a bitter cold day, and when we noted that morning that the field was practically frozen, Ray Flaherty suggested we use rubber-soled sneaker shoes instead of cleats.

Ray came from the state of Washington, and remembered a game out that way in which the winners had used sneakers to run wild. Cleats will not grip but will skid on hard-frozen ground. The rubber soles on sneakers afford traction.

That morning we tried to find a store open to buy sneakers. Failing, we gave up the idea. But coming on to half time, I had the clubhouse boy call up Abe Cohen, a tailor who served as locker room attendant for Manhattan College, a few miles north of the Polo Grounds. Abe was to meet my messenger at the gym and let him have all the sneakers available. Abe didn't have a key, so the lockers were busted open. He looted nine pairs.

In the meantime, back at the Polo Grounds, my brother Bill had gone out on sneakers, and reported the smooth-soled shoes would be perfect, because the field had frozen tight. If it hadn't and there had been slime and mud spots here and there, we would have been hung up, because part of the gridiron would support cleats, and part sneakers, so that there wouldn't be an advantage in wearing either.

Our boys got on the sneakers, and as we walked down the clubhouse stairs we saw the Bears taking an interest in our footwear. Walt Kiesling, who was on that team, told me later that George Halas, coach, advised his gang to step on our toes, and that would fix us for wearing sneakers.

Ken Strong lost the toenail of his big toe kicking off in tennis shoes, but that was all we lost in the second half. The Bears had whipped us twice that season, by 27–7 and 10–9, but the sneakers made it our day, by 30–13, for one of the big upsets in the history of the league.

I have always had a particular kick out of boys who showed an aptitude for coaching and who later made good in that line. Joe Kuharich was one. He was on the Cardinals, after graduating from Notre Dame, and I got acquainted with him when he played for me on several All-Star squads. Joe was smart, and he was one of the few linemen in the league who ever called the offensive plays. I took quite a liking to Joe, and recommended him for the coaching job at San Francisco U. He was successful there, and moved up to become coach of the Cardinals.

I guess you get the idea that I think big-league football is fine. By and large, it has never disappointed me in that belief. I know of only one time anything in the game made me mad and sick and worried. That was the time in 1946, just before we were to meet the Bears in the Polo Grounds for the world championship, that two of our boys, Frank Filchock and Merle Hapes, were accused of having to do with gamblers.

That thing broke Saturday afternoon, the day before the big game. The Maras and I were called to the mayor's residence in Gracie Square, and then we went to police headquarters, where we dug into the thing to get at the truth.

One Alvin Paris, who later was sentenced to prison, was charged with having offered a bribe to Hapes to influence the outcome of the game with the Bears. Filchock knew of this offer but did not report it. Worst of all, both boys had associated with this Paris and his crowd—you know, bright lights and smart entertainment.

The police had Paris as well as the two boys in for questioning, and you might say Paris was in no hurry to co-operate.

I said to Commissioner Arthur W. Wallander: "If you will let me take this so-and-so into the inspector's room for a few minutes, while you look the other way, I guarantee I'll get his confession."

Wallander looked at me, with a tight little grin on his face, and answered: "I believe you would, Steve, but you know I can't let you do it that way."

Finally, it was disclosed that neither boy was criminally involved. But there was no doubt that Hapes, although he did not take a bribe, had led Paris on by permitting the fixer to wine and dine him.

Filchock was just plain foolish for not telling what he knew, the minute he knew it.

The police cleared the boys, and that put a decision up to Bert Bell, commissioner of the league. Hapes had gone too far to be permitted to play football, and the commissioner so ruled. In the case of Filchock, he permitted him to play against the Bears, and no one ever saw a boy give a more spirited and courageous performance on the football field. Honestly, it choked you up, knowing how hard he was trying. The Bears defeated us, 24–14, but it was not for lack of effort by Filchock. The boy's nose was broken early in the game, but he kept on fighting through every play with blood and mud coating his face and uniform. In his heart he hoped the past would be forgotten.

But Bell in the end banned Filchock as well as Hapes, and that was the only way, because a game such as ours cannot exist if anyone connected with it gives rise to any suspicion, however innocently, of wrongdoing.

Aside from that unhappy incident, I have always been proud of our game and of the boys who play it. Except for that tragic episode, there has never been the shadow of doubt on our sport.

I always thought professional football presented a wonderful opportunity to boys just graduated from college. I remember my first year with the Kansas City Cowboys. When I got home after that season, I was able to pay off $350 I had borrowed to complete my schooling. A few years later I wasn't so smart. I stepped off the bus in my home town at that time, Kinsley, Kansas, pretty well beaten down. After a twenty-game season of league and exhibition games, I was a little older but not a bit wiser, because I was just where I was six months earlier. I hadn't saved a penny, and I had been making good money for those days. I didn't know where the money had gone. A few clothes I didn't need, a few losses at poker, a dollar here and a dollar there that I didn't need to spend. I decided I had been a chump to work so hard and wind up with nothing to show for it.

The following fall I opened a bank account in New York, and I took a great pride in that little black book as the years went on. I still make our boys start accounts in that bank, near our hotel. Now I get a big kick out of seeing them line up on paydays to sock their money away.

Pro football is no good for a boy who regards it as a career. That boy is just no good for pro football. He is going to be a drifter, and that kind of boy is not reliable.

College boys who have football talent often ask my advice about playing professionally. I tell them if they have ability and size and love of the game, okay. But they must play football in our league only if they have a purpose for later years. They should save money, plan for a master's degree, get next to a good job that will stand up for them after they make a pile in three to five years of football. Football, I tell them, can give them a great start—but only a start. They must provide the finish.

Professional football isn't a profession, and shouldn't be regarded as such. It is a stepping stone for a fellow with ambition.

On one of my squads I had twenty-six out of the thirty-three boys going back to school after the season for various specialized courses which would better fit them to make their living when they retired from football. Through the years I have been proud of my boys, for their good common sense in looking to the future, and in making successes of themselves.

Take the off-season activities of the squad of 1951. Charley Conerly put his money into a cotton farm back home in Mississippi. Joe Scott has a cattle ranch in Texas. Joe Sulaitis and Al DeRogatis got onto good jobs in New York, which they have held several years and which offer advancement. Arnie Weinmeister started an insurance business in Seattle. So did Otto Schnellbacher in Topeka and Forrest Griffith in Kansas City. Also in Kansas City, Johnny Amberg has an interest in a clothing business. Johnny Rapacz, Stonewall Jackson, and Bob Hudson are going on with school. Bob Wilkinson worked in the movies as a stunt man and finally earned a featured role. Travis Tidwell does radio work in Birmingham. Eddie Price likes to work with kids and is a supervisor of playgrounds in New Orleans.

Herb Hannah started a dairy farm in Ball Ground, Georgia. Bob McChesney has a position in an aircraft firm on Long Island. Kelly Mote bought a farm in Georgia. Harmon Rowe is in plumbing supplies in California, and

Tom Landry is studying advanced practice in industrial engineering. Kyle Rote is a building contractor in Corpus Christi, Texas. Dick Woodard sells agricultural implements in Davenport, Iowa. John Cannady is a restaurant proprietor in Charleston, South Carolina. Tex Coulter ranks high as a sports cartoonist and works for a paper in Dallas, Fritz Barzilauskas is a partner in an auto agency in Connecticut. Ray Kraus and Emlen Tunnell are salesmen. If there are any missing, it's not because they are not employed, but because I've just forgotten to put down their names. Every single member of our '51 squad had an off-season occupation which was promising for the boy's future.

In fact, that outside business often becomes so profitable and important that a coach loses a boy a year or two before he ought to. That hurts, but I don't have much comeback when a boy comes to me and says his business is so good he is retiring from football. That's just what I've been telling him all the while.

There is one outside item, however, which I would like to complain about right now. That's babies. You have no idea how the coach has to struggle through with players who are going to be dads when football season is coming up. Sometimes I have to take up a boy and remind him that the Giants front office really is not responsible for the babies born to the squad.

A word or two about conduct of players in the season. We have very few rules. Gambling is not permitted, although rummy or hearts as pastimes are all right, because a card game like that relaxes. We don't allow drinking and will not argue about that. A boy who is caught drinking is through—that's the end for him right on the spot.

We very seldom have bed checks, and do not have a curfew. If the boys don't get their proper rest, I'll know

[232]

that on the field. As a rule I believe in encouraging these men to stand on their own, to have pride in their position, and to realize the value in taking care of themselves.

I believe these kids understand that when they cheat they are not fooling the coach. They are merely cheating themselves and their teammates.

You will find, on the squads in our league, that the boys have a very high sense of morale, as well as morals. They will not put up with a fellow who won't stay in line and who isn't giving value for the money he accepts. That kind of boy gets a fast chill, and, if he doesn't respond, he can't last long.

I have no patience with people who say the pros don't play football, and that they don't have the spirit the college players have. Those people don't know what they are talking about, and they certainly don't have any understanding of human nature. What they are saying is that the college heroes who had spirit one year don't have it the next, just because they become professionals. Well, you just can't change character overnight that way, and a fellow with backbone and integrity doesn't lose the two no matter what he does or how long he lives.

Personally, I feel professionals have more incentive than college boys, without meaning to run down the latter in any way. Our boys are older, they have a more mature grasp of what they are aiming for. They have a purpose in football. They are making their living. They must have a thought for those babies I mentioned. Their earning power depends directly on what they put out.

We don't want bums, and, since we have the choice of players, you can bet we are going to take the guy with ambition. Naturally, he is going to be a better player than the drifter. Pro football never made a bum out of a boy who didn't have the idea in mind much before he joined up with us. You will find bums in high school and college as well as everywhere else humans congregate. We are in position to get rid of any bum we might pick up.

Pro football players had no finer testimonial than in the last war, when fully 75 per cent of the men who entered service became officers. Some who were drafted got as high as captain. The Army, the Navy, and the Marines are just as choosy as we are about men in responsible positions, and they paid our boys a wonderful compliment.

It's been a long happy trip through the years for me since I got off that bus in Kinsley, with the folks knowing little about my game, except that it couldn't be much if I showed up broke. Nowadays when I get back home, the folks know all about professional football. They respect it, and are glad to see me. They hear it on the radio, they have a knowledge of the players, and every now and then a fellow will dig out a couple of issues of the *Sporting News* which he has saved, and quiz me about articles which that paper carries on the pros during the football season. That's a thrill, which comes because of the tremendous strides my game has made in a brief period of twenty years.

I remember back to the day in 1927 when we were heading for the world championship, and only eighty fans showed up at the Polo Grounds to see us play the Bears. I remember when Mr. Mara brought me and the Cowboys all the way from Duluth to New York, and drew only $1,800 at the gate. Today the guarantee a visiting team gets is $20,000, and its share can go up over $40,000 for a big game.

All the effort and all the money that has been poured into this game has in the end chiefly benefited the players. The All-America Conference helped in that respect, and also in publicizing football in places where it had not been known or seen. Due to competition in recent years, players have seen their wages skyrocket. They have been able to dicker for bonuses and for three- or four-year contracts, instead of going along from year to year.

Big-league football was never so sound or so important to so many fans as it is today. And it never was more rewarding to those in it. I have no criticism to make. But I do have a suggestion, about a move I would like to see made soon. I would like to have the game of football uniform for the fans, so that they would have identical rules governing the action wherever it is, on sandlot, in high school, on college campus, or among the pros. I do not see any reason why the various rules-making bodies cannot get together to achieve this sensible goal.

The pros have always been friendly to the colleges. We have a rule, to begin with, which prevents us from signing a college boy until his class has graduated. We don't want to interfere with any boy's education, and we held to this rule, although it hurt us many a time, when the rival All-America Conference in a way got around it a few years back.

We don't gloat over the things which have happened recently in college ball, which haven't helped anybody. We are sorry. The only thing I wish the high-school and college coaches would do is abandon the two-platoon system, because I believe a boy, when he is learning the game, should have a right to see both sides of the picture, so that he may become a well-rounded player, not a kid who may always have a blind spot in the game. Show the boy both offense and defense, and then it is time enough for him to specialize.

I believe that when we pros create a fan, or when college ball creates a fan, he is a fan for all football, and should be presented the same game no matter where he sees it. Football has a place in our way of life. The game has never caused great harm, and many fine things have come out of it. But for heaven's sake, let's all play the same kind of football.

As it stands, the High School Federation and the pros agree on more points than either does with the colleges, without good reason. The high schools adopted the forward pass rule, as we know it today, very soon after we did and much before the colleges.

In defense of the main differences the pros show with the colleges, I believe our version will stand critical scrutiny.

We have our goal posts on the goal line; colleges put these on the end line in 1925, ten yards back, and never restored them to their traditional position. We believe, and can prove, that our goal post position discourages ties, which are popular nowhere.

As for the possibility of injury with posts on the line, Pop Warner had the answer for that. "In all my experience," he would say, "the only one I ever saw hurt by goal posts was one of those damn fools who tear 'em down after the game is over."

We bring the ball in bounds twenty yards for the start of every play, and the colleges place it a few yards nearer the side line. In either case the offense has room to use either side, so what's the difference? Why can't the rule be uniform, through compromise if necessary?

I do not think the college rule on a grounded ball is as thoughtful as ours. In college a ball-carrier, even if he is in the open, is downed if his body touches the ground. We say a man who may slip in the open has a right to get up and continue, unless, in the opinion of the official, he is about to be tackled. Contrary to common belief, we do not encourage injuries by allowing a man who is tackled to try to get up and run. If he is in the grasp of an opponent when he falls, he is downed.

The college rule which prohibits running with a fumble is not in the tradition of sports as we know it, because it does not permit the opponent to take full advantage of a mistake. In any game of skill, a man should pay the full penalty for his mistake. We permit running with the ball, and I feel that is a fair as well as an exciting part of the game.

We have worked up to a substitution rule which speeds up the game and avoids times out and penalties for subbing, because we can change men at any time, provided the thirty-second rule in putting the ball in play is observed.

Our rule of thirty seconds from the time the referee spots the ball until the center snaps it is five seconds longer than the college period. But the average time of putting the ball in play among the pros is only twenty-one seconds. We want the thirty seconds available to take account of an occasional mix-up, or subbing, so as to avoid a penalty that slows the game. The time is there if needed, but it is seldom required. In recent seasons the pros have been packing sixty minutes of football into a shorter elapsed time than ever in history.

Why can't we all get together and draw up one code of rules for football, to benefit the player, the fans, and the promotion of the sport? I am looking forward to that enlightened day.

Right now, after going on like this through so many pages, it's time I recalled a fitting story from early Oklahoma when I was growing up. It's a tale which has a point right here.

There was a couple down the road from our house who were tremendously proud of the way their infant was learning to talk. Time and again I remember the dad holding up his child in pride while it mumbled that baby language which only fond parents understand.

This went on about a year or so, and by that time the kid had learned to talk so well that it never was still. One day our family stopped off at that couple's house, and nobody could speak for very long without the young heir butting in.

The dad squirmed around a while, and then he got up, pointed a finger at the child, and shouted:

"Now that you've learned to talk—shut up!"

Index

Rowe, Harmon, 124, 186, 198, 231
Russell, Bo, 111
Russell, Rusty, 132

S

Sanders, Red, 132
Schnellbacher, Otto, 91, 124, 175, 198, 231
Scott, Joe, 189, 197, 231
Scott, Ralph, 76
Shaffer, Leland, 3, 202, 219
Shaughnessy, Clark, 131
Single wing, 132, 152
Sinkwich, Frank, 121
Smith, Frank, 200
Smith, Willis, 16
Soar, Hank, 174, 203, 219
Speedie, Mac, 125, 150, 182, 209
Split line, 155
Split T, 131, 188
Spread formation, 132
Stanford University, 131
Stecher, Scissors Joe, 57
Stedham, Tom, 17
Sternaman, Joey, 17
Strader, Red, 145
Strauss, Dutch, 45
Stribling, Bill, 199
Strong, Ken, 82, 202, 219, 228
Stydahar, Joe, 100
Sulaitis, Joe, 24, 231
Sutherland, Jock, 31, 122, 183
Sweeny, Miriam, 99
Swiacki, Bill, 96, 197

T

T formation, 131, 149
Tatum, Jim, 132
Taylor, Hugh, 150
Texas University, 14
Thompson, Tommy, 149
Thorpe, Jim, 28, 50
Tidwell, Travis, 198, 231
Tierney, Jim, 85
Todd, Dick, 149, 216
Toledo Maroons, 28, 45
Topping, Dan, 197
Trippi, Charlie, 153
Tunnell, Emlen, 14, 119, 176, 197, 232
Tuttle, Orville, 203, 218

U

Umbrella defense, 186
Ustler, Herb, 30

V

Van Buren, Steve, 182, 213
Viberg, Ernie, 129

W

W. & J. University, 33
Wallander, Arthur W., 229
Walls, Will, 101, 146, 203, 218
Walsh, Adam, 148
Warner, Pop, 128, 236
Washington Redskins, 96, 111, 146, 156